AN EYE FOR AN EYE

"For none can tell to what red Hell
His sightless soul may stray."

—*Ballad of Reading Gaol.*

AN EYE FOR AN EYE

BY

CLARENCE S. DARROW

*Author of "Farmington," "Resist Not Evil,"
etc., etc.*

THE LAWBOOK EXCHANGE, LTD.
UNION, NEW JERSEY
1996

ISBN 1-886363-07-2

Printed in the United States of America
on Acid-Free Paper

Please see catalogue at rear of this book
for other titles reprinted by:

The Lawbook Exchange, Ltd.
965 Jefferson Avenue
Union, New Jersey 07083-8605

AN EYE FOR AN EYE

BY

CLARENCE S. DARROW

Author of "Farmington," "Resist Not Evil,"
etc., etc.

NEW YORK
FOX, DUFFIELD & COMPANY
1905

Published September, 1905

THE PREMIER PRESS
NEW YORK

AN EYE FOR AN EYE

AN EYE FOR AN EYE

I

WHEN Hank Clery left the switch-yards in the outskirts of Chicago he took the street car and went down town. He was going to the county jail on the north side of the river. Hank had never been inside the jail though he had been arrested a number of times and taken to the police court, escaping luckily with a small fine which his mother had contrived to pay. She was one of the best washerwomen of the whole neighborhood, and never without work. All the officers knew that whenever Hank got into trouble his mother would pay the fine and costs. Hank had often been arrested, but he was by no means a bad fellow. He lived with his old Irish mother and was very fond of her and often brought his wages home if none of the boys happened to be near when the pay-car came around. Hank was a switchman in one of the big railroad yards in Chicago. Of course, he and his companions drank quite a little, and then their sports and pastimes were not of the gentlest sort; for that matter neither was their work—climbing up and down running cars and turning switches just ahead of a great locomotive and watching to make sure which track was safe where the moving cars and engines were all around—did not tend to a quiet life. Of course, most people think that no man will work in a switch-yard unless he drinks. Perhaps no man would drink unless he worked in a switch-yard or some such place.

Well, on this day Hank was going to the jail, not on account of any of his own misdeeds, but on an errand of mercy. The night before, the priest had come to Hank's home and told him that his old friend, Jim Jackson, had begged for him to visit the jail. Hank at first refused, but the priest told him that Jim had no friends and was anxious to have a few minutes' talk with him before he died; Jim had some message that he wanted to give Hank that he could not leave with any one else. Hank knew that Jim was to be hanged on Friday, and he had thought about it a good deal in the last few days and wished that it was over. He had known Jim for a long time; they had often been out together, and sometimes got drunk together. Jim once worked in the yards, but one night one of the other boys was struck by the Limited as it pulled out on the main track, and Jim and Hank gathered him up when the last Pullman coach had rolled over him; and after that Jim would never go back to the yards; so he managed to get an old horse and wagon and began peddling potatoes on the street.

One evening Hank took up the paper, and there he saw a headline covering the whole page and a little fine print below telling how Jim had killed his wife with a poker. Hank did not understand how this could be true, but as the evidence seemed plain he made up his mind that Jim had really always been a demon, but that he had managed to keep it hidden from his friends. Hank really did not want to go to the jail to see Jim; somehow it seemed as if it was not the same fellow that he used to know so well, and then he was afraid and nervous about talking with a man who was going to be hanged next day. But the priest said so much that finally Hank's mother told him she thought he ought to go. So he made up his mind that he would stand it, although he was a great deal more afraid and nervous than when he was turning switches in the yard. After the priest left the house Hank went down to the alderman and got a pass to go inside the jail. He always went to the alderman for everything; all the people thought that this was what an alderman was for and they cared nothing about anything else he did.

When Hank got down town he went straight across the Dearborn street bridge to the county jail. It was just getting dusk as he came up to the great building. The jail did not look a bit like a jail. It was a tall grand building, made of white stone, and the long rows of windows that cover the whole Dearborn street side looked bright and cheerful with the electric lights that were turned on as Hank came up to the door. If it had not been for the iron-bars across the windows he might have thought that he was looking at a bank or a great wholesale warehouse. Hank stepped into the large vestibule just inside the shelter of the big front door. Along each side was a row of people sitting on benches placed against the wall. He did not wait to look closely at this crowd; in fact, he could not have done so had he tried, for Hank was no artist or philosopher and was neither subtle nor deep. He saw them just as he would have seen a freight-car stealing down the track to catch him unawares. He did notice that most of these watchers were women, that many of them were little children, and that all looked poor and woe-begone. They were the same people that Hank saw every day out by the yards, living in the rumble of the moving trains and under the black clouds of smoke and stench that floated over their mean homes from the great chimneys and vats of the packing houses. Most of the women and children had baskets or bundles in their arms, and sat meek and still waiting for the big key to turn in the great iron lock of the second door.

When Hank went up to this door some one inside pushed back a little slide, showed his face at the peep-hole, and asked him who he was and what he wanted. Hank shoved the alderman's letter through the little window and the door opened without delay. This was not the first time that the gloomy gate had turned on its hinges under the magic of that name, both for coming in and going out.

Inside the little office was the same motley, helpless crowd of people, the same sad-faced women and weary children standing dazed and dejected with their poor baskets and bundles in their arms. Some were waiting to be taken through this barred door, while others had just returned and were stopping until the turnkey should open the outside gate and let them go.

In a few minutes a guard came to Hank and asked if he was the man who brought the alderman's note. On receiving the reply, the guard told him that the alderman was all right and it was worth while to be his friend. That was the way he got his job and he always stuck by his friends. Then the guard unlocked another door and took Hank to the elevator where he was carried to the fourth story. Here he was let off on an iron floor directly in front of a great door made of iron bars. The turnkey quickly unlocked and opened this door and let Hank and the guard into what seemed a long hall with iron floor, ceiling and walls. Nothing but iron all around. Along one side of the hall were more iron bars, and a wire netting ran from the ceiling to the floor. Along the whole length of this wire netting was a row of the same kind of people Hank had seen below. They were packed close to the grating, and crowding and pushing to get up to the screening. Most of these were women, here and there one of them holding a little child by the hand and one with a baby in her arms. On the other side Hank saw a row of men pressing just as closely to the netting, most of these looking pale and ill. The evening was hot and not a breath of fresh air was anywhere about. The peculiar odor of the prison, more sickening than the stock-yards stench which Hank always breathed, was so strong that he could not tell whether he smelled it or tasted it.

The guards were rushing noisily around among

the visitors and inmates, passing bundles and baskets out and in, calling the names of the prisoners to be taken from their cells inside and brought down to the wire netting to get a glimpse of some relative or friend. Hank was bewildered at it all and for a few minutes stood almost dazed, wondering what it meant and what good purpose it all served.

Next to him stood a woman, perhaps forty years of age; in one hand she held a basket, and by the other the hand of a little girl about nine years old. The woman was dressed in a loose, ill-fitting gown and on her head was a black sailor hat. Behind the wire-screen was a man of about her own age. He wore only black trousers, suspenders, a grayish woolen shirt and old shoes. The man and woman stood with their fingers touching through the netting. Hank heard the man say that he did not know what to do, that the good lawyers charged so much that he couldn't have them, and the ones who came to the jail did more harm than good. It was funny that you couldn't do anything without a lawyer. One of the prisoners, who was a smart man and had been there a good many times, had told him that the best way was to plead guilty and ask the mercy of the court; that he thought the judge might let him off with a two hundred dollar fine—"you know the State's Attorney gets the money." Hank heard the woman answer that maybe to pay the fine was the best way after all; as soon as he was arrested she took Gussy out of the high school, and Gussy was now working in the department store and thought Aggie could get in as a cash girl; of course Aggie was too young, but still she was pretty large for her age and might get through, as Gussy knew the floor-walker very well—he stopped at the house to visit one evening that week and was real nice.

"I've been scrubbing in the Masonic Temple nights, but it's pretty hard work and I am getting so large I am afraid I can't keep it up much longer. You know I'll be sick next month. There are a few things in the house yet and I might get a a little money on them, and then there are the Maloneys next door; you know we were always fighting, but after you went away they seemed kind of sorry and have been awfully good to us, and I think they might help us a little, although they haven't got much themselves——"

Hank couldn't stop to hear all they said, and besides he felt as if he had no right to stand and listen, so he let his eye wander on down the line. Just beyond he saw an old bent, gray-haired woman with a long black veil and spotless black gown. She was crying and talking to a young man inside the grating. He heard her ask, "How could you have done it?" and heard him answer, "Mother, I don't know, but somehow I didn't seem to think about it at the time." Just beyond were a man and a woman and it was so hard for them to get close to the screen that the man held a little baby up in his arms to look over the people in front. The child looked in wonder and then held out its hands and shouted with delight, "Mamma, there's papa. Papa, have you been here all the time? Why don't you come back home?" Young girls, too, pressed closely up to the screen, each with that look at the youth inside that neither the wise nor the foolish have ever failed to understand. The prison bars and the laws that placed their lovers outside the pale had no power to change their feeling, only to deepen and intensify their love.

While Hank stood in the corridor a number of men called from the inside: "Pardner, have you got any tobacco?" Hank hastily gave away all he had, and thought that if he should ever come back he would buy as much as he could before his visit. But his musing was soon interrupted by the guard tapping him on the shoulder and telling him he was ready. Then another turnkey opened a barred door and let him inside the wicket. Here he stood in a narrow hallway with still another big locked door in front. Soon this was swung open, and at last Hank stood inside the bars and the nettings with a great throng of coatless, hatless men all talking, laughing, chewing and smoking, and walking by twos and threes, up and down the room. Hank had always supposed that these men were different from the ones he knew and had fancied that he would be afraid to be with such a crowd, but when he got inside, somehow he did not think of them as burglars and pick-pockets; they seemed just like other men, except that they were a little paler and thinner and more bent. Some of these men spoke to Hank, asking him for tobacco or for money. He saw one man whom he knew very well, one of his neighbors that he supposed was out of town; and he quickly noticed that this man tried to keep out of his sight. Hank had never thought that he was bad, and could not but wonder how he happened to be here.

Hank looked around for Jim, but was told that he was upstairs locked in his cell. The guard explained that the death-watch had been set on him and that for some time no one had left him day or night. He was to be hanged in the morning before sunrise. He himself had gone around that day and handed written invitations to the judges to be present. Some of them had asked him whether they could get in a few friends who wanted to go and see the hanging. The guard said they had over a thousand applications for tickets; that it was one of the most popular hangings they'd ever had in the jail. He supposed this was because Jackson had killed his wife and the newspapers had said so much about it.

He could not help feeling sorry for Jackson. Of course, he supposed he was awfully wicked or he wouldn't have killed his wife, but since he had come to know Jackson he had found him a perfect gentleman and very kind and obliging, and he acted like a good fellow. It really seemed kind of tough to hang a man. He had seen a good many men hung and was getting kind of tired of it. He believed he would go out in the country fishing somewhere to-morrow instead of staying to see it done. They never needed so many guards on that day because all the prisoners were kept locked up in their cells.

As Hank went along, the guard chatted to him in the most friendly way. He pointed over to the court-yard where there were some long black beams and boards, and said that was where they were going to hang Jackson, that the carpenters would put up the scaffold in the night. The murderers' row where Jim was kept was around on the side where he couldn't see the carpenters put up the scaffold. It used to be right in front but it had been changed. The guard said he didn't see much difference, because the men could hear it and they knew just what it was, and anyhow they never could sleep the last night unless they took something. He told Hank that after they got through he would take him down to the office and show him a piece of the rope that they used to hang the Anarchists, and the one they used on Pendergast, who killed Carter Harrison, and the one they had for the car-barn murderers. It was the very best rope they could get; some people wouldn't know it from clothes-line but it was a good deal finer and more expensive.

The guard said it was strange how these men acted before they were hanged.

"You wouldn't hardly know them from the prisoners who were in jail working out a fine," he explained. "They don't seem to mind it very much or talk about it a great deal. Of course, at first they generally kind of think that the Supreme Court is going to give them a new trial; their lawyers tell them so. But half the time this is so that their friends will get more money to pay for carrying the cases up; though I must say that some of the lawyers are good fellows and do all they can to help them. Sometimes some of the lawyers that have the worst reputations are really better than the others. Then after the Supreme Court decides against them, they have a chance to go to the governor and the Board of Pardons. Of course this isn't much use, but somehow they always think it will be, and the case is never really decided until the last day and that kind of helps to keep them up. Now, there's Jackson; I took him the telegram about an hour ago and he read it and it didn't seem to make much difference. He just said, 'Well, I s'pose that's all.' And then he picked it up and read it again and said, 'Well, the lawyer says he's going back to the governor at midnight. Something might happen then; will the office be open if any telegram comes?' I told him that it would and he says, 'Well, I presume that it's no use; but where there's life there's hope.' I s'pose the lawyer just said that to kind of brace him up and that he took the night train back to Chicago, but I didn't tell Jim so. Well, anyhow, I'm going to see that he has a good breakfast. We always give 'em any thing they want, either tea or coffee, ham and eggs, bacon, steak, beans, potatoes, wheat cakes and molasses, almost anything you can think of. Of course most of 'em can't eat much, but some of 'em take a pretty big breakfast. It really don't do any good, only the taste of it goin' down; they are always dead before it has a chance to digest. A good many of 'em feel rather squeamish in the morning and drink a good deal before they start out. We always give 'em all they want to drink; most of 'em are really drunk when they are hung. But I think that's all right, don't you? There were some temperance people once that made a row about it, but I think that's carrying temperance entirely too far myself.

"Well, I didn't mean to gossip with you so much, but I thought maybe you would like to know something about it and so long as the alderman sent you over I wanted to do all I could for you. Give my respects to the alderman. I guess he'll be a candidate next spring. He says he won't, but I think he will. He always knows what he's doing. All he wants is to throw them reform guys off the track. They might know that they couldn't beat him. Our people out there don't care anything about municipal ownership and Civil Service Reform, and things like that. What they want is turkeys on Thanksgiving and to be helped out of the lock-up and pardoned out of the Bridewell and found jobs. That's what they want, and there ain't an alderman in town that tends to the business of his ward better than ours, and we don't care whether the railroads and gas companies give him money or not. We don't expect him to work for nothin' and don't want him to; and what do we care about the streets? None of us has horses and the fellows that wants 'em ought to pay for 'em. Well, here's Jackson, and I'll tell the guard to let you stay with him all you want to; he's a good fellow and will do what I want. You can say anything you please to Jackson and he can talk to you all he wants to; the guard won't listen if he knows you're all right, but it isn't any more than fair, anyhow, for this is his last night."

Hank listened to the guard without being impatient for, in the first place, he felt as if he had made a new friend, and he liked him; he was such a good talker and told him so much that was new and he didn't seem the least bit stuck up, although he had such a good job. Then all the time he felt nervous and uneasy about meeting Jackson; the Jackson he knew was not a criminal but a good fellow who used to play pool and drink beer and go to primaries, while this man was a murderer who was to be hung next day; then again he didn't seem a real man, but a sort of ghost, so that Hank had a good deal the feeling he used to know as a child when he went past a grave-yard, or that he felt in a morgue, or when he went to look at some dead friend.

When he came up to the cell Jackson was smoking a cigar and talking with the guard. At the first glance the uneasy feeling passed away. It was the same Jim Jackson that he knew, except thinner and paler than when he saw him last. Before the guard had time to speak Jackson reached out his hand, smiled and said "Hello, Hank, I'm awful glad you came. I've been looking for you all the afternoon." Hank took his hand without the least feeling that it was the hand of a murderer. It was only the old friend and comrade he had known.

The guard unlocked the door and told Hank to go in. Then he said:

"Now, you folks talk all you want to. I won't hear a single word you say. I'll sit out here and if there is anything I can do, let me know."

Hank went into the little cell. On one side was an iron shelf and on this a straw tick and some bed clothing. A little wash-stand and slop-pail stood in one corner, a chair was near the stand, and a few pictures taken from colored supplements were on the white walls. The guard handed in another chair and the two friends sat down. At first there was a short, painful silence. It was plain that both had been thinking what to say and neither knew just how to begin. Hank had thought that he would ask Jim how he happened to kill his wife; he thought he ought to talk with him and tell him how terrible it was. He believed that perhaps this was his duty toward a fellow-being standing so near the presence of his Maker. Then, too, he had the feeling that unless he really told Jim what he thought about his crime, it would be almost the same as being an accessory to the act. In fact, when Hank was going to the jail he had a vague idea that his only right to visit Jim was to preach to him in some way. He would almost have thought it a crime to meet him on equal terms.

After they sat down Jim was again the first to speak. "My room here's pretty crowded but I guess it'll do for to-night. Make yourself just as comfortable as possible for I'd like to have you stay with me as long as you can. It's a little lonesome you know. The guard's a good fellow. He visits with me every night and is as friendly as he can be. He told me that he was in jail himself once for burglary, but you mustn't say anything about it. His lawyer got him out, but he says he was really guilty. That was a good many years ago. He says he believes if he had gone to the penitentiary he would never have amounted to anything, but as soon as he got out of jail he turned over a new leaf and made up his mind to make something of himself, and just see where he is now. He is an awful kind fellow. I know he feels sorry for me. He gives me all the cigars I want and all the privileges he can. There's a guard here in the daytime that I don't like; he was appointed by the Citizens' Association. He's strict and awful good. He's always asking me questions about myself, says he's getting statistics for the association. He seems to think that it must have been whiskey that made me do it, and he gives me tracts; of course that's all right, but still you'd think that once in a while he'd say something else to a fellow, or at least give him a cigar. Some way he don't seem to have any feeling. I s'pose he's a good deal better than the other guard but I don't like him near so well.

"But that wasn't what I got you here for. I really wanted to talk with you. You see no one that I knew has been to see me since I came. I don't s'pose I ought to expect they would. I used to know a good many fellers who went to jail but

I never went to see 'em. I always kind of thought they wa'n't fit for me to associate with, and I s'pose that's the way most people believe. But since I came here somehow it don't look quite the same. Maybe that's on account of what I done. I told the priest I thought you'd come because we was always such good friends, and he told me he would go and see you. He's been awful good to me although I never went to church any when I was out. He talks to me as if I was just like other people. Of course he tells me I done wrong, and I know I did, but he don't tell me as if I was the only one that ever done wrong, and as if he and every one else was so much different, and as if he couldn't see how I done it. He talks just as if my soul was worth as much as anybody's and as if I'd have a better chance afterward than I ever had before. Anyhow he's done me lots of good and I honestly believe he's made me a better man, and if I only had a chance to do anything now I'd amount to something; but of course I can't. But still, I wanted to tell you a few things that I couldn't even tell him, for you know that, no matter how good he is, he somehow seems different from you; you know I kind of feel as if you was just like me. You'll excuse me, I know, for saying this, bein' as the time is so short.

"You remember about my boy. Now of course I always was a rough fellow and never did quite right ever before that, but still I guess you know I always loved that kid. Strange thing, he'll be four years old to-morrow on the very day—well, poor little fellow, I hope he don't know nothing about it. You remember the time that kid had the croup and how we thought he couldn't get well, and you know I went down to the yard to tell you about it and how bad I felt. I almost wish now he'd died, but maybe that's wicked and God will take care of the kid better'n he did of me. Well, I haven't heard a word about that boy since I came to the jail, or since I left him at the house that night, except a little bit in court and what that good guard says. He kind of holds out that he's in some kind of an orphan-asylum where he's gettin' plenty to eat and where he'll learn what's right and wrong, and be a good man, and that's all right, but I'd like to know where the kid is. He says if I thought so much of him I ought to have showed it before, and I s'pose I ought; but I did think lots of him; just as much as them rich folks think of their boys. I want him to be taken care of and to be educated and grow up to be a good man, and maybe it's a good deal better if he never knows anything about his father, but somehow I can't help wantin' him to know who I was and don't want him to think of me just like the newspapers and everybody else does. I wouldn't want him to grow up like that guard, even if he is real good. And you see there wa'n't any one but you that I could send for and tell them just how it all happened. No one yet has ever known how it was, and everybody says I was to blame and that I'm a demon and a monster, and I thought maybe if I explained the whole thing to you, just as it was, you could see that I wa'n't so much to blame; anyhow that there was some excuse for what I done, and then some time when the boy's growed up he'd know that I wa'n't so bad as every one says I was.

"Of course I know you can't, for I know you're poor like me, but so many times when I thought about the boy I thought that maybe you and your mother might raise him just the way I would have done; and then your mother was always so good to all of us. I remember how she used to raise the little geese down along the canal if anything happened to the old goose; don't you remember about that? My, but them was fine times, wa'n't they? Of course if you could do it I don't know but the alderman would help you; anyhow he'd get free books and clothes off'n the county when he went to school. How are politics up in the ward? Is he goin' to run again? I never hear anything only what I get out of the papers and they're all against him, but I think he'll show 'em yet. Wish I was out so I could help. But I must go on with what I brought you to hear. I'm goin' to tell you the whole story just exactly as it is, and you know that I wouldn't tell you a lie to-night with what they are goin' to do in the mornin'. I can't make you understand unless I commence clear at the beginnin', but I know you won't mind, seein' it's my last time."

II

"You know I was born in Chicago and never was out of it but once until the night it happened. I don't know anything about my father and mother except what my aunt told me. You know she raised me, and I can't make any complaint about the way she done it. I was real small when I went to live with her. She stayed all alone down on the canal. I guess you knew me when I was livin' with her. She worked hard, but, of course, ladies of that kind don't get much. She used to go over to the south side to do washin' and to clean houses, and things like that, and sometimes when I was small she took me along. They were awful nice houses where we went. That's how I got to know so much about the way rich people live. When I got bigger, she used to send me to school. I was pretty steady in school and got clear up to the sixth grade. I know it must have been awful hard for her to send me the way she earnt her money, but she seemed to think as much of me as if I'd been her own boy. She could have got along better, but every time she got five or ten dollars laid up it seemed as if there was a funeral of some of the neighbors and she had to club in and hire a carriage, and that took her money almost as fast as she could earn it.

"You remember how we used to play around the canal in them days. It smelled pretty bad but we didn't seem to mind it much. We used to sail boats and go in swimmin' and catch frogs and do most everything. There was quite a gang of us boys that lived there. It don't seem as if any of 'em ever amounted to very much. Most of 'em are in the stock yards or switchin' or doin' somethin' like that. The only ones that I can think of that growed up down there and amounted to anything is the alderman and Bull Carmody, who went to the legislature. They call both of 'em Honor'ble, you know. I guess anybody is honor'ble who ever had an office or tried to get one. Us boys used to get arrested quite a good deal. Of course we was pretty tough, you know that. We was always in some devilment. All of us rushed the can and chewed tobacco; then we fought a good deal and used to play 'round the cars. Some of the boys would break into 'em; but I never stole anything in my life unless you count coal off'n the cars, and I don't know how we could have got along in the winter without that. Anyhow I guess nobody thinks anything of stealin' coal off'n cars.

"But I don't s'pose there's any use goin' over my whole history. I don't know as it has anything to do with it anyway, only it kind of seems to me that I never had a very good chance and as if mebbe things would've been different if I had.

"Well, you remember when my aunt died I had got to be about fourteen. Then I found a job out to the stock yards. I never liked that work; I used to see so much killin'. At first I felt sorry for the cattle and the hogs, and especially for the sheep and calves—they all seemed so helpless and innocent—but after I'd been there awhile I got used to seein' their throats cut and seein' blood around everywhere, all over the buildings and in the gutters, and I didn't think any more about it. You know I stayed there quite a while. Then I went to work for the railroad company. First I was in the freight house unloadin' cars. This was pretty rough, heavy work, but I didn't mind it much; you know I was always kind of stout. Then I thought I'd like to work in the yards; it would give me more air and not be quite so confinin'. So I got a job as switchman, same as you. Well, you know all about that work. It ain't the nicest thing in the world to be a switchman. Of course, if they'd make the couplers all alike then there wouldn't be so much danger; but you know when one of them safety couplers comes against one of the old kind that the boys call "man killers" it's pretty dangerous business. Then, of course, when a car is run down a switch and you have to couple it onto another car just as it bumps in, it's kind of dangerous too. Of course, the rules say you must use a stick to put the link into the draw-head, but nobody ever uses a stick; you know all the boys would laugh at a feller that used a stick. There ain't nothin' to do but to go in between the cars and take hold of the link and put it in. If anything happens to be wrong with the bumpers and they slip past, of course you get squeezed to death; or, if you miss the link, or it gets caught or anything, your head or arm is liable to be smashed off. Then you've got to watch all the time, for if you stub your toe or forget for a second, you're gone. I kind of think that the switch-yards make a feller reckless and desperate, and I don't believe that a man that works in the switch yards or stock yards looks at things quite the same as other people. Still you know them fellers ain't bad. You've seen 'em cry when they went home to tell a lady how her man had been run over, or tell some old woman about how her boy had got hurt, and you know we always helped the boys out and we didn't have much money either.

"You remember we was workin' together in the yards when the strike come on. I was in debt, just as I always have been. Somehow I never could keep out of debt; could you? The rich people say it's because we drink so much, but I'd like to see them try to live on what we get. Why, you know we hardly ever go to the theatre, and if we do we go up in the gallery. I never had a job of work done on my teeth in my life except once when I paid a quarter to get one pulled. Do you s'pose any of us would ever think we could get a gold fillin' in our teeth? Now that suit of clothes over on the bed is the first whole suit of new clothes I ever had. The guard brought 'em in a little while ago, and I'm to put 'em on in the mornin'. But I guess they won't do me much good. I'd rather they had taken the money and give it to the kid for a rockin' horse or candy.

"But I was tellin' about the strike. My, the way I go on! I guess it's because this is the first time I've had a chance to say anything to any one since it happened, and of course it'll be my last. As soon as I got back my lawyer told me not to talk to any one, but I don't see what difference it would have made—them detectives seemed to know everything and a good deal more, they knew more about me than I ever knew about myself.

"You remember all of us went out on the strike. I guess most of the boys was in debt, but they all struck just the same. The papers abused us and said we hadn't any right to strike; that we hadn't any grievance, and it was worse for us to strike on that account. Now it seemed to me that it was better to strike for the Pullman people than for ourselves—it didn't seem so selfish; but the papers and the judges didn't look at it that way. Of course the strike was pretty hard on all of us. I got into the lock-up before it was over, though I never meant to do nothin'. I guess I did hit a scab over the head, but he was comin' to take our job. It's queer how everybody looks at things a different way. Now I never thought it was so awful bad to hit a scab who was takin' another man's job. Of course I know some of 'em are poor and have families, but so have the strikers got families and we was strikin' to help all the poor people. If you read the newspapers and hear what the judges say you would think hittin' scabs was worse'n murder. I don't s'pose it's just right, but I don't hardly see what else is to be done. You remember that scab, don't you, that worked with us on the road, and you remember when he got his leg cut off, and how all the boys helped him, and the railroad fought his case and beat him, and yet they always seemed to think more of him than any of the rest of us. Now it seems to me there's lots of things worse'n hittin' scabs. If I was one of them packers I know I'd give a lot of meat to poor people instead of fixin' every way I could to make 'em pay so much, but the rich people don't seem to think there's anything wrong about that, but it's awful to hit a scab or to strike.

"Well, you know after the strike was over none of us could get a job anywhere, but finally I changed my name and managed to get in again. I believe the yard master knew who I was and felt kind of sorry for me. Anyhow I got the job. Then you know the time Jimmy Carroll got run over by that limited train. I sort of lost my nerve. I wouldn't have thought about it if all the cars hadn't run over him; but when we had to pick up his head and his legs and his arms and his body all in different places, I somehow got scared and couldn't switch any more. So I quit the yards. But I've been runnin' along so over things that really don't have anything to do with the case that I've almost forgot the things I wanted to tell you about. But just wait a minute; I hear some one comin' down the corridor and I want to see who it is. No, it's only one of the guards. I didn't know but possibly my lawyer might have sent—but I guess it's no use.

"Let me see; I was goin' to tell you about gettin' married. You knew her, Hank. You remember when we got a job again after the strike and you know the little restaurant where we used to board? Well, you remember she was waitin' on the table. All the boys knew her and they all liked her too; she was always real friendly and jolly with all of us, but she was all right. Of course she couldn't have got much wages there for it was only a cheap place where the railroad boys et, but somehow she always seemed to keep herself fixed up pretty well. I never thought much about her, only to kind of jolly her like the rest of the boys, until that time she got that red waist and done her hair up with them red ribbons. I don't know anything about how it was, but them seemed to ketch my eye and I commenced goin' with her, and used to get off as early as I could from the yards, and when she got through washin' the supper things we used to go out and take street-car rides, and go for walks in the parks, and stay out late almost every night.

"Finally I made up my mind that I wanted to

settle down and have a home. Of course I knew t'would be more confinin', but then I thought t'would be better. So one night when we was out walkin' I kind of brought it 'round some way and asked her to marry me. I was surprised when she said she would, because she was so much nicer than me or any of the rest of the boys; but she said she would right straight off, and then I asked when it had better be and she said she didn't see any use waitin', so long as it was goin' to be done. Of course, I hadn't thought of its comin' right away, and I wa'n't really prepared because I was considerable in debt and would like to've paid up first. I told her how I was fixed and she said that didn't make any difference, that she'd always heard that two could live as cheap as one, and that she was savin' and a good manager and it wouldn't cost us much to start, for she'd noticed the signs in the street cars about four rooms furnished for ninety-five dollars with only five dollars down, and we wouldn't need but three rooms anyway. Then, after I'd asked her to marry me and had made up my mind to do it there wa'n't no excuse for waitin', so the next Sunday we went over to St. Joe and got married. She asked me if I didn't think that was just as good as any way.

"When we come back we rented three rooms down near the yards for ten dollars a month, and went down to the store to buy the furniture, but the clerk made us think that so long as we was just startin' and I had a good job we ought to get better things than the ninety-five dollars, so we spent one hundred and fifty dollars and agreed to pay ten dollars a month, and the furniture was to be theirs until it was paid for.

"Well, we started in to keep house and got along pretty well at first. She was a good housekeeper and savin' and I kind of liked bein' married. Of course, it cost us a little more'n I expected, and when I came to buy clothes and shoes and pay grocery bills I found that two couldn't live as cheap as one, but I hadn't any doubt but that she thought they could. I guess all women does. Then I got hurt and was laid off for two months and couldn't pay the installments, and got behind on my rent, and got in debt at the store, and this made it pretty hard. When I went to work I paid all I had, but somehow I never could catch up.

"Well, about that time the kid was born, and then we had to have the doctor and I had to get a hired girl for a week, for I wanted to do everything I could for her, and that all kept me back. Then they commenced threatenin' to take the furniture away, and every week the collector came 'round and I did all I could, but somehow I couldn't make it come out even.

"I s'pose you don't see what all this has got to do with my killin' her, and I don't think I quite see myself, but still I want to tell it all. Sometimes I think if I hadn't been so poor and in debt I never would have done it, and I don't believe I would. I was so much in debt that I felt sorry when I knew we was goin' to have the child. I didn't see how we could bring it up and make anything out of it, and how it could ever have any better chance than I had. And then she'd been doin' a little work to help out on the furniture, and I knew that she couldn't do any more after that. But still as soon as the child was born I was always glad of it, and used to think more about him than any one else, and I would have done anything I could for it. She liked him too, and was always good to him, and no matter what I say about her I can't say that she didn't treat the boy all right.

"Well, after the kid was about a year old we began to have trouble. She was always complainin' that I didn't bring home enough money. She said I went 'round too much nights and that I drank too much beer and chewed too much tobacco and smoked too much, and she complained most all the time, and then I got mad and we had a row. I don't mean to blame her, 'specially after what happened, and since I've been here so long doin' nothin' but countin' the days and waitin' for my lawyer to come, I've had time to think of ever'thing a good deal more than I ever did before. And I don't say she was to blame. I s'pose it was hard for her, too. Of course, the rooms was small and they was awful hot in the summer and cold in the winter, and then the collectors was always comin' 'round, and I used to be tired when I got home, and I was so blue that I said things without really knowin' that I said 'em. Ain't you done that when somebody was talkin' to you and your mind was on somethin' else, kind of answered 'em back without knowin' what they said or what you said? I presume I was cross a good many times and mebbe it was as hard for her as t'was for me. Of course, I used to wish I'd never got married and that I was boardin' back there to the restaurant when I didn't have all the debts; and I s'pose she'd been better off back there too, waitin' on the table; anyhow she always looked better in them days than she did after we was married, so I guess she must have got more money at the restaurant than I gave her. But after the boy was born I never really wished we wa'n't married, for I always thought of him and knew he never would have been born if we hadn't got married; but of course, that didn't keep us from fightin'. I don't mean that we fought all the time. Sometimes when I got home she was as nice as she could be, and had supper all ready, and we'd read the newspaper and talk and have a real good time; but then, again somethin' would happen to put us out and we'd fight. I can't say that she always begun it. I guess I begun it a good many times. I found fault because the bills was too big and the way things was cooked, and the way she looked, and, of course, if I said anything she got mad and answered back. I've thought a lot about our fights and that awful one we had last, and I don't believe one of 'em would have happened if it hadn't been for the money. Of course, I s'pose other people would make some other excuses for their fights and that no one would be to blame if you would let 'em tell it themselves, but I'm most sure that if I'd only been gettin' money enough to keep a hired girl and live in a good place, and get good clothes and dress her and the boy the way they ought to have been, and not get in debt, we wouldn't have fought.

"The debts kep' gettin' bigger all the time and I begun to get scared for fear the furniture would be took away—we hadn't paid more'n half up and then there was a good deal of interest. I went one day to see a lawyer, but he didn't tell me anything that done me any good and I had to pay him ten dollars out of my next month's wages, so that made me all the worse off. Lawyers get their money awful easy, don't they? I always wished I could be a lawyer and if I had my life to live over again I would be one if I could.

"It seemed as if things kep' gettin' worse at home and I stayed out a good many nights because I didn't want a row for I knew there'd be one as soon as I got home. So far most of our fightin' had been only jawin' back an' forth. Once she threw a dish at me and I slapped her in the face, but didn't hurt her, and I guess she didn't try hard to hit me with the dish; anyhow if she had wanted to she was near enough so she could.

"One night though, I come home pretty late. I'd been out with the boys to a caucus and we had drunk quite a bit. The Alderman was running again and had got us a keg of beer. I didn't really know what I was doin' when I came in. I was hopin' she'd be in bed but she was waitin' for me when I come in and said: 'There comes my drunkard again. This is a pretty time of night to get home! You'd better go back to your drunken cronies and stay the rest of the night,'— and a lot of more things like that. I told her to shut up and go to bed, but that made her madder and then she called me a lot of names. I told her to stop or I'd choke her, but she kep' right on talkin', callin' me a drunkard and all kinds of names, and tellin' me how I'd treated her and the boy; I couldn't make her keep still; the more I threatened her the more she talked. Finally she said, 'You cowardly brute, I dare you to touch me!' and she kind of come right up to where I was. Of course I didn't really half think what I was doin', but I drawed off and hit her in the face with my fist. I guess I hit her pretty hard; anyhow she fell on the floor, and I ran up to her to pick her up, but she said, 'Leave me alone, you coward,' and then I was madder'n ever and I kicked her. The next day she went to the police court and had me arrested. The judge was awful hard on me, told me if he had his way 'bout it he'd have a law made to have wife-beaters whipped with a cat-o'-nine tails in the public square, and he fined me one hundred dollars.

"Of course I hadn't any money so I went to jail, but in a day or two she went to the judge and cried and told him I was all right when I wasn't drunk and she got me out. I never thought that judge done right to lecture me the way he did. I don't think that strikin' your wife is as bad as strikin' your child, and still most everybody does that. Most women can defend themselves but a little child can't do anything. Still, of course, I don't defend strikin' your wife, only one word kind of brings on another and it sounds different in the newspaper from what it really is.

"Well, after I got home from the jail we talked it over together and made up our minds we'd better part. Things had gone so bad with us that we thought it wa'n't worth while to try any more and mebbe we'd both be better off alone. She was real sensible about it and was goin' to keep the boy. I promised to give 'em half my wages and was to see him whenever I wanted to.

"When we got our minds made up we went to see about a lawyer. She'd been goin' over to the Settlement a good deal for advice and they'd been good to us but they didn't like me; they blamed me for ever'thing that happened, and of course them settlement ladies wa'n't none of 'em married and they couldn't understand how a feller would drink or fight with his wife. They didn't know what allowance a woman has to make for a man, same as a man does for a woman —only a different kind. When she told 'em what we were goin' to do they all said, 'No, you mustn't do that. You must make the best of it and stay together'; they said that even if I promised to give her half my money I never would do it, but would go off and she'd never see me again. If they knew anything about what I thought of the boy they wouldn't have said it. Then they said it would be a disgrace and that it would disgrace the child. I wish now we'd done it anyway. It would have been better for the child than it is now. Then she went to see the priest. We were both born Catholics, although we hadn't paid much attention to it. That was the reason we went to St. Joe to get married. The priest told her that she mustn't get a divorce, that divorces wa'n't allowed except on scriptural grounds. Of course we couldn't get it on them grounds. There never was nothin' wrong with her—I'll always say that—and as for me I don't think she ever suspected anything of that kind. Even if I had wanted to I never had any money, and besides I've had to work too hard all my life for anything like that. Then when I went to the lawyer he said it would cost fifty dollars, but I hadn't any fifty dollars. So we made up our minds to try it again. I don't see, though, why they charged fifty dollars. If a divorce is right a man ought not to have it just because he's got fifty dollars when a poor man can't get it at all.

"It was a little better for a while. We both had a scare and then when we talked of quittin' I s'pose we thought more of each other. Anyhow we'd lived together so long that we'd kind of got in the habit of it. But still it didn't last long; I don't believe 'twas right for us to stay together after all that had happened and the way we felt and had lived up to that time. If we'd only separated then—but we didn't, and it's no use talkin' about it now.

"It was just about this time that Jimmy Carroll was killed and she didn't want me to work in the yards after that. She was 'most as 'fraid as I was so we made up our minds that I'd quit. It was then that I went to peddlin'; but wait a minute before I tell that, let's go and speak to the guard."

The two men got up and went to the iron door and looked out through the bars at the shining electric lights in the corridors. The guard sat near the door talking with the prisoner in the next cell. He looked up and put two cigars through the grates.

"Is there anything I can do for you, Jackson?"

"No, I guess not. Nothin' more has come from him, has there?"

"No, but it's early yet."

"Well, I guess it's no use."

The men looked out a moment at the iron corridor and then lighted their cigars and sat down. Hank could hardly speak. Somehow this simple contact with his old friend had driven away all the feeling of the crime that he had brought with him to the jail. He no longer thought of him as Jackson, the wife-murderer, but as Jim, the boy he once knew and the man that had worked in the switch-yards and grown up by his side.

Out in the street they heard a steady stream of carriages and the merry laugh of men and women passing by. Hank listened to the voices and asked who they were.

"Oh, the people drivin' past in their carriages to the theatre. You know all the northside swells drive down Dearborn Avenue past the jail. I wonder if they ever think of us in here, or if they know what is goin' to be done to-morrow. I s'pose if they do they think it's all right. What a queer world it is. Do you s'pose one of them was ever in here? Well, I don't believe I'd be either if only I'd had their chance."

The two men sat stripped almost to the skin; the putrid prison air soaked into Hank at every pore. The sweat ran from his face and he felt as if the great jail were a big oven filled with the damned and kept boiling hot by some infernal imps. Here and there along the big corridors they heard the echo of a half demoniac laugh, a few couplets of a ribald song, and the echoing sound of the heavy boots of a guard walking up and down the iron floor. Silently they smoked their cigars almost to the end and then Jim again took up his story.

III

"When I made up my mind to quit the railroad I looked 'round for somethin' else to do. It was kind of hard times just then and a good many men were out of work and I couldn't find anything that suited me. Of course I never had much schoolin' and t'want every kind of job I could hold anyhow. I went back out to the stock yards, but they was layin' off men and there wa'n't anything there. One mornin' I went over to see Sol Goldstein. He was a nice old man that we used to buy potatoes of. He told me that he was gettin' so old and kind of sick that he thought he'd have to give up peddlin' and let his boys take care of him the rest of his time. He said he didn't think it would be very long anyhow, and they could do that much for him so long as he'd done so much for them. He said as I hadn't any job why didn't I buy his horse and express wagon and go to peddlin'. I could take his license, that hadn't run out yet, and go right along over his route. I told him I hadn't any money to buy his horse and wagon with, but he told me that didn't make any difference, I could pay for 'em when I earnt the money. So I made a bargain; got the horse and wagon and harness and two old blankets for fifty dollars. Of course they wa'n't worth much; the horse had a ringbone and the heaves and kind of limped in one of its hind legs. Goldstein said that was on account of a spavin, but he told me there was another one comin' on the other hind leg and as quick as that got a little bigger he'd stop limpin' because he couldn't favor both hind legs to once. Goldstein said the ringbone had been killed and the heaves wouldn't bother him much. All I had to do was to wet the hay before I fed him. So I bought the rig. I didn't know nothin' about horses but I knew what Goldstein said was all right for we'd been friends a long time.

"I went down to Water street and bought a load of potatoes and went to work. I haven't time to tell you all about my peddlin'; anyhow it ain't got much to do with the case, not much more'n any of the rest. My lawyer always said any time I told him anything, 'Well, what's that got to do with your killin' her,' and the judge said about the same thing whenever we asked any questions. He couldn't see that anything I ever done had anything to do with it except the bad things. He let 'em prove all of them and they looked a good deal worse when they was told in court and in the newspapers than they seemed when I done 'em. I guess there ain't nobody who'd like to hear every bad thing they ever done told right out in public and printed in the newspapers. I kind of think t'would ruin any one's character to do that, 'specially if you wa'n't allowed to show the good things you'd done.

"I hadn't been peddlin' very long until an inspector asked me for my license and I showed it to him, and he said that it wa'n't any good, that I couldn't use Goldstein's license; that it was just for him, and that I must stop peddlin' until I went down to the City Hall and paid twenty-five dollars for another one. I didn't know where to get the twenty-five dollars; anyhow I don't see why any one should have to pay a license for peddlin'; nobody but poor people peddles and it's hard enough to get along without payin' a license. Anybody don't have to pay a license for sellin' things in a store and I don't think it's fair. But I went and seen the alderman and told him about it, and he said he could get it fixed and to go right on just as if nothin' had happened and if any one bothered me again to send 'em to him. So I went right ahead. I don't know what he done but anyhow I wa'n't bothered any more until Goldstein's license had run out.

"Peddlin' is kind of hard work. You've got to get up before daylight and go down and get your potatoes and veg't'bles and things, then you have to drive all over and ask every one to buy, and most people won't take anything from you 'cause you're a peddler and they're 'fraid you'll cheat 'em. Of course we do cheat a little sometimes. We get a load of potatoes cheap that's been froze, and then again we get a lot of figs that's full of worms and roll 'em in flour and then sell 'em out, but all figs is full of worms, and I guess most everything else is, even water, but it's all right if you don't know or think anything about it. And of course, half of the year it's awful hot drivin' 'round the streets and the other half it's awful cold, and sometimes it rains and snows and you get all wet and cold, and it ain't very healthy either. Most peddlers have the consumption, but then there's lots of poor people has consumption. It's funny, too, about where you can sell stuff; you'd think you ought to go where people has got money but this ain't no use; they never will buy nothin' of peddlers and they won't even let you drive on their high-toned streets, even after you've paid a license. If you want to sell anything you've got to go among the poor people. Of course they can't buy very much, but then they pay more for what they get. It's queer ain't it, the way things are fixed; them as works hardest has to pay the most for what they eat, and gets the poorest stuff at that. Did you ever go and look at one of them meat-markets on the south side? Do you s'pose that they'd take any of the meat that's in ours? They might buy it for their dogs and cats but they wouldn't eat it themselves.

"Once in a while I used to take the kid along with me when I was sellin' things, and he always liked to go, but if it commenced to rain or turned cold I had to go back with him, and then he always got tired before night. So I didn't take him very often. I kind of laid out to take him when she done the washin', so he'd be out of her way, and he used to kind of like to drive and I amused him a good deal that way.

"I think mebbe I made about as much peddlin' as I did on the railroad, but not any more, after I paid for my horse feed and the rent of the barn and gettin' the wagon and harness fixed once in a while. Anyhow I didn't get out of debt any faster, and the furniture men kept threatenin' me until I went to one of them chattel-mortgage fellers and borrowed the money and mortgaged all I had and paid five dollars for makin' out the papers and five per cent. a month for the money. This didn't seem like so very much but it counts up pretty fast when you come to pay it every month. Then one day my horse up and died. I didn't know what was the matter with him. He seemed all right at night and in the mornin' he was dead. I didn't know what to do at first so I went and seen the alderman. He gave me a letter to some men who run a renderin'-plant and I went out there and bought an old horse for five dollars. It was one they was goin' to kill, and it seemed too bad to make him work any more; still I guess he'd rather work than be killed; that's the way with people and I guess horses is about like people. I always thought that horses had about the worst time there is; they can't never do anything they want to, they have to get up just when you tell 'em to and be tied in a stall and eat just what you give 'em and depend on you to bring 'em water. Even when they're goin' along the road they can't turn out for a mud hole but have to go just where you want 'em to and never have a chance to do anything but work.

"This horse wa'n't much good but I managed to use him in my business. The boys would holler at me and ask me if I was goin' to the bone-yard or the renderin'-plant, and once or twice one of the humane-officers stopped me and came pretty near takin' it away and killin' it, but nobody ever saw me abusin' it, and I fed it all I could afford. I remember one night in the winter, about the coldest night we had, I heard it stampin' and I couldn't go to sleep. I knew it was stampin' because it was so cold. We didn't have any too much cover ourselves, but it worried me so much I got up and went out to the barn and strapped an old blanket on the horse and then came back and went to bed. I guess this was the other horse though, the one that died, for I didn't have this last one over a winter. But I don't know as it makes any difference which horse it was.

"Well, I can't tell you all about my peddlin', it ain't worth while, and I must go on and tell you about how it happened. It was on the 26th day of November. You remember the day. There's been a lot said about it in the newspapers. It was just three days before Thanksgivin'. I remember I was thinkin' of Thanksgivin', for we'd been livin' pretty poorly, not very much but potatoes, for it was a rather hard fall on all us poor folks. I always hated to take the money for the things I sold but I couldn't help it. You know I couldn't give things away as if I was Rockefeller or Vanderbilt. Well, I knew we was goin' to get a turkey from the alderman Thanksgivin', just two days later, and I should have thought that would have cheered me up, but it didn't. That mornin' it was pretty cold when I got up. It was the first snow of the season, one of them blindin', freezin' days that we get in November, and then, of course, I wa'n't used to the cold weather and wa'n't dressed for it either. I didn't have much breakfast for we didn't have much stuff in the house. She got up and fried some potatoes and a little pork and that was about all, and then I hitched up the old horse and drove away. No one else was on the street. There wa'n't generally, when I started after my loads in the mornin'. The old horse didn't like to go either; he kind of pulled back on the hitch strap when I led him out of the barn, the way you sometimes see horses do when they hate to go anywhere or leave the barn. I s'pose horses is just like us about bein' lazy and sick, and havin' their mean days, only they can't do anything about it. Well, I went down and got my load. In the first place I had some trouble with the Dago where I got the potatoes; they were pretty good ones but had been nipped a little by the frost in the car, and he couldn't have sold 'em to the stores, at least to any of the stores on the north side or the south side. They was just such potatoes as had to go to us poor folks and most likely to peddlers, and he wanted to charge me just about as much as if they was all right. I told him that I'd have some trouble in sellin' 'em and I ought to make somethin' off'n 'em. He said I'd get just as much as I could for any kind, and I told him that I might possibly, but if I was goin' to pay full price I wanted my customers to have just as good potatoes as any one got, and besides I might lose some of my customers by sellin' them that kind of potatoes. Then he dunned me for what I owed him and threatened not to trust me any more and by the time I left with my load I was worried and out of sorts, and made a poor start for the day.

"Well, I drove over along Bunker Street, among the sheeneys, and commenced calling 'po-ta-to-es.' Nobody much seemed to buy. A few people came out and picked 'em all over and tried to jew me down, and mebbe bought half a peck. I don't know how they thought I could make any money that way. Still the people was all poor; most of 'em worked in the sweat-shops and hadn't any money to waste on luxuries. I worked down Maxwell Street and things didn't get much better.

It seemed as if everybody was out there sellin' potatoes, and it was awful cold, and I hadn't any coat on, and the horse was shiverin' every time we stopped. Of course I always put the blanket on him if we stayed long, but the blanket was pretty old and patched. Then I drove down south, where the people lives that work in the stock yards. It went some better down there but not very much; anyhow I didn't get any warmer. Along toward noon I hitched the horse under a shed and gave him a few oats and I went into the saloon and bought a glass of whiskey and took four or five of them long red-hots that they keep on the counters. They tasted pretty good and I never stopped to think what they was made of; whether they was beef, or pork, or horse, or what, though you know everybody always says they work in all the old horses that don't go to the renderin'-plant and some that does, but they was good enough for me and was hot, and when I went away I felt better and I guess the old horse did, too. Well, I drove on down around the streets and did the best I could. I remember one place where an old lady came out and said she hadn't had anything to eat since yesterday and there wa'n't nothin' in the house, and I up and gave her half a peck, though I couldn't hardly afford to do it. You know that half a peck was more to me than it is to Rockefeller when he gives a million to the school, but my lawyer wouldn't let me prove it when I tried; he said the judge would only laugh if he ever mentioned it. The newspapers never printed a word about it either, although I kind of thought it might lighten up the people's feelin' some and help me a bit; but they did prove all about the time I struck her and some other things I wa'n't on trial for, although my lawyer objected all he could and said I wa'n't on trial for 'em, which I wa'n't; but the judge said no, of course I wa'n't, but they'd show malice, so they went in and was printed in the newspapers, and the jury looked awful at me, but I bet every one of 'em had done most as bad. When I gave the old woman the half peck of potatoes she called on all the saints to bless me to the end of my days. I felt kind of better as I went away, and thought mebbe they'd do somethin' for me, and this wa'n't more than seven or eight hours before it happened.

"Of course, most folks would think that any one like me wouldn't have given away a half a peck of potatoes, but they don't really understand them things; you've got to do a thing before you can know all about it. If I was makin' the laws I wouldn't let any one be on a jury and try a feller for murder unless he'd killed some one. Most fellers don't know anything about how any one kills a person and why they do it, and they ain't fit to judge. Now, of course, most everybody would think that any one who had killed any one, unless it was in war or somethin' like that, was bad through and through; they wouldn't think that they could ever do anything good; but here I give away that half peck of potatoes just because I knew the lady was poor and needed 'em—and I see things every day here in jail that shows it ain't so. Just a little while ago one of the prisoners was took down with small-pox and every one was scared, and another prisoner who was in here for burglary went to the ward and nursed him and took care of him, and took the disease and died. And most all of the fellers will do anything for each other. The other day there were five fellers on trial for robbin' a safe, and the State's Attorney done all he could to get one of 'em to tell on another feller who hadn't been caught or indicted, and he promised every one of 'em that he wouldn't do a thing with 'em if they'd tell, and he couldn't get a word out of any of 'em, and they went to the penitentiary, just because they wouldn't tell; and the State's Attorney and the judge all of 'em seemed to think that if they could get one feller to tell on some one else that he'd be the best one of the lot and ought to be let out. If you'd just stay here a few days and see some of the wives and fathers and mothers come into the jail and see how they'd cry and go on over some of these people, and tell how good they was to them, it would open your eyes. They ain't one of them people, unless it's me, that don't have some one that loves 'em, and says they've been awful good to 'em and feel sorry for 'em and excuses 'em, and thinks they're just like everybody else. Now there was them car-barn murderers that killed so many people and robbed so much. Every one wanted to tear 'em to pieces and no one had a single good word for 'em, but you'd ought to seen Van Dine's mother and how she hung onto her boy and cried about him and loved him and told how many good things he'd done, just like any one else; and then that Niedemeyer, who tried to kill himself so he couldn't get hung, you know he went to a detective and confessed a lot of crimes, so that the detective could get the money after he was hung, and the detective agreed to divide the money with his mother. If you was here a while you'd find these fellers doin' just as many things to help each other as the people on the outside. It's funny how human nature is, how anybody can be so good and so bad too. Now I s'pose most people outside can't see how a murderer or a burglar can do anything good any more than the poor people down our way can see how Rockefeller can charge all of us so much for his oil and then give a million dollars to a church or a school.

"There was a feller came over here to the jail to talk to our Moral Improvement Club and he had some queer ideas. Most of the prisoners rather liked what he said and still they thought he was too radical. I never heard any such talk before and I don't quite see how they let him do it, but I've thought about what he said a good deal since then and think mebbe there's somethin' in it. He was a good deal different from the other ones that come. Most of 'em tell us about our souls and how we can all make 'em white if we only will. They all tell us that we are a bad lot now; but he kind of claimed that the people inside the jail was just like the people outside, only not so lucky; that we done things because we couldn't help it and had to do 'em, and that it's worse for the people on the outside to punish the people on the inside than to do the things we done. Now, I hain't had anything to do but think about it and what I done, and it don't seem as if I could help it. I never intended to kill anybody but somehow everything just led up to it, and I didn't know I was gettin' in to it until it was done, and now here I am. Of course, when I was out I used to rail about these criminals and think they was awful bad just the same as every one else did, but now I see how they got into it too, and how mebbe they ain't so bad; even them car-barn murderers,—if they'd been taken somewhere out west on a ranch where they could have had lots of air and exercise and not put in school, which wa'n't the place for boys like them, I believe they'd 've come out all right and been like most other boys and sobered down after they got older. I really think if they'd been taken away they'd 've tried to be good and if they'd been given plenty of exercise, like herdin' cattle and things like that, mebbe it would have been just as good as to kill 'em. Anyhow there was them Younger boys and Frank James who killed so many people and they are out now and all right. Nobody's afraid of 'em and they won't likely never do anything of that kind any more.

"But I'm gettin' clear off'n my subject again, just as I always am. I was tellin' you about that day. Well, after I gave the lady the half peck of potatoes I went on peddlin', but didn't seem to sell much. I ought to 've got through by two or three o'clock. It was a long enough day for me, and the horse, too, but I had so many potatoes left that I couldn't stop, so I kept on. I got down around Thirty-fifth Street and was pretty cold and went into a saloon where I saw one of the boys. One of 'em was runnin' for the legislature and he asked us all to take a drink, and of course we did; then he asked us to take another and we done that; and in a few minutes that feller that was runnin' for the senate, he come in and he asked us all to take a drink and of course we done that, and he said a few words about the election and how he hoped we all would vote for him, and we told him we would, and that as near as we could find out all the boys was with him, that the other feller was a kind of stiff anyhow. He went out, and then, just as I was leavin', the feller that was runnin' against him, he come in and he set 'em up a couple of times and said he hoped we was all with him, and of course we told him we was, and then he went away. Well, of course, I took whiskey every time because I was cold and that kind of warmed me up. Then I went out to the wagon again and drove on down Thirty-fifth Street to sell the rest of the potatoes. Finally the horse began to go lame, and seemed pretty tired, and I turned back toward the house, peddlin' on the way. I guess I didn't sell anything after I left Thirty-fifth Street, though I kept callin' out until my voice got kind of husky and all stopped up. I guess it was the cold air that I wa'n't used to yet. The snow was comin' down pretty fast as I drove along and the wind was blowin' quite a bit in my face and it was a bad night. It commenced gettin' dark pretty soon after. You know the days are short along the last of November.

"Then I kep' thinkin' about the cold weather. I always hated winter anyhow, and I hadn't expected 'twould turn cold quite so quick and of course I wa'n't ready for it. I couldn't seem to think of anything but the winter. I s'pose that was the reason I done the things I did afterward. I got to thinkin' about the house and how many cracks there was in it and how much coal it took to heat it. Then I began to think about the price of coal and how it's cheaper in the summer than in the winter, and how the price keeps goin' up so much a month all the time until winter, so, of course, all the rich people can get their coal in the summer when it was cheap and leave the poor people to get it in the winter when it got high. Then I thought how everything seemed to be against the poor and how you couldn't get on no matter what you done.

"I hadn't got my potatoes more'n two-thirds sold out and I didn't have any good place to keep 'em. I couldn't afford to take chances of 'em gettin' frost-bitten any more. You know how easy potatoes freeze. You have to watch out while you're peddlin' 'em in the fall and winter and some days you don't dare take 'em out at all. Before I got home I thought I'd have another drink so I stopped at a saloon where they always had the pollin' place and where a good many politicians usually hung out; and I found some of the boys there, and the fellow that was runnin' for assessor was in the saloon. He asked us all to drink a couple o' times, and then he told us how easy he was in assessin' the poor people's property, and asked us to vote for him. We all said we would, and then he told us how he was assessor last year and how he'd stuck it onto the rich people and the corporations and how they was all against him this year. We all liked that, and then he gave us another drink. I was gettin' so I felt it just a little, but of course I wa'n't drunk. I could walk all right and talk pretty straight. I don't suppose I'd taken more'n ten or twelve drinks in all day, and you know that won't hurt anybody. I don't know what I would've done such a cold day if it hadn't been for the drinks. Oh, yes, in the last place they got to talkin' about the alderman and said as how he wa'n't goin' to give out any turkeys this year. I didn't like that and some of the other fellers didn't like it. He'd already got elected and had been givin' 'em to us and we didn't see what right he had to quit. They said the reason he wa'n't goin' to give 'em was because a lot of the fellers had quarelled about 'em and then some of 'em had taken his turkeys and voted the other ticket, and some people had found fault with him because they didn't get any turkey, and it looked as if he was losin' votes instead of makin' 'em. Well, I'd been dependin' on the turkey and it made me feel a little blue, for I didn't know how I was goin' to get anything for Thanksgivin', and I didn't think that you could have much of a Thanksgivin' just on potatoes and mebbe a little pork. So I wa'n't feelin' none too good when I got on the wagon and drove away from the last place. It seemed as if everything had turned against me and I didn't know what I was goin' to do. It's funny how much difference luck makes with a feller. You know somethin' can happen in the mornin' and make you feel good all day, and then again somethin' will go wrong and no matter what you are doin' it seems as if there was a sort of a weight pullin' down on you. Well, I felt kind of blue as I drove home. I don't think I could hardly have kept up only for the whiskey I'd drunk. I was kind of wonderin' what it was all for and I didn't see any reason for anything, or any chance that anything would be any better, or any real reason for livin'.

"Before I went to the house I drove up to the barn and unhitched the horse and led him in, and then I run the wagon in, and took the potatoes out and put 'em under a little bag of hay that I had in the corner, and threw the horse blanket over 'em. Then I unharnessed the horse and bedded him down and gave him some hay and a little oats. I'd watered him at one of the last places I stopped—one of them troughs they have in front of saloons. Then after I got the horse tended to I went into the house."

Hank got up and went to the door and spoke to the guard. He was still sitting on the stool and talking to the prisoner in the next cell. Once more he handed Hank a cigar.

"Give one to Jim," he said. "I can't do much more for him, poor devil; I'm awful sorry."

Jim came up and took the cigar and looked down at the guard.

"I don't s'pose nothin' has come for me, has there?"

"No, not yet," was the answer.

"Well, I presume it's no use."

Just then the noise of pounding and driving nails and low voices was heard over in the court yard.

"What's that?" Hank asked.

"Don't you know! That's the fellers buildin' the scaffold; they always do it the night before. Strange, ain't it; somehow it don't seem to me as if it was really me that was goin' to be hung on it; but I s'pose it is. Now, isn't it strange about the governor; just one word from him could save my life. I'd think he'd do it, wouldn't you? I s'pose he don't really think how it seems to me. I know I'd do it, no matter what any one had done.

"But it's gettin' late and I must go on with my story or I won't get it finished before—before you have to go. It's pretty hard to tell all 'bout this part, but I'm goin' to tell it to you honest and not make myself any better'n I am. I've thought about this a good deal when I've tried to account for how I done it, and I guess I can tell everything that happened. When I look at it now it seems years ago, almost a lifetime, not as if it was last November. I guess it's because so much has happened since then. It seems, too, as if it wa'n't me that was doin' it, but as if t'was some one else. I guess that'll make it easier for me to tell; anyhow, I want you to know how it was, and then some time you can tell the boy, if you think it's the right thing to do."

IV

"I FORGOT to tell you about the steak. I don't see how I left that out, for, really, that's what caused the whole trouble. It beats all what little things will do, don't it? Now, lots o' times in my life it has seemed as if the smallest things had the most to do with me. There was that red waist, for instance, that she wore that day she was waitin' on the table. I 'most know I never would have paid any attention to her if it hadn't been for that red waist. And then that beefsteak—in one way I'm goin' to get hung on account of that beefsteak. How many times since that I've just wished I hadn't stopped and bought it. But you see I was feelin' cold all day, and when I come 'round Thirty-fifth Street the wind kind of got in my face worse'n it had done before, and it sort of struck me through the chest too; my legs didn't feel it quite so much, because they had the blanket over 'em. Well, just as I got up to the second corner there was a saloon right in front of me. This was before I got to the corner when I met the senators, and I thought I'd go in and get a drink; and then right on the other side was that meat-market and there was a lot of chickens and steak and things hangin' in the window, and they looked mighty good, for I hadn't had much to eat all day. At first I thought I'd go and get a drink, and then I thought I could get enough steak for supper for just about what the drink would cost, and the steak would do the most good, and besides she and the kid could have some of that, and I thought it would make her feel pleasanter and liven her up a bit. We hadn't been gettin' along any too well for some time.

"So I pulled up the horse a minute and went into the shop and asked the butcher about the steak hangin' in the window, and he told me that it was sixteen cents a pound and that it was a sirloin steak. I thought that was most too much and asked him if he hadn't some cheaper kind. He said yes, that a rump steak was just as good, and he showed me one of them and the whole piece came to fifteen cents—just the price of a glass of whiskey—and I bought it and rolled it up in a piece of brown paper and went away.

"Now I was tellin' about this to the good guard that likes to get statistics for the Citizens' Association, and I told him it was the beefsteak that brought me here, and that if I had only got the whiskey instead of the steak it wouldn't have happened, but he argued the other way, and then when I stuck to my story he got kind of mad about it and said it was them drinks I had with the senators and the assessor that really done it, and if it hadn't been for the drinks I'd have known better, and he said he was goin' to put it down that way, and I'm sure he did. I hain't no doubt but a good many of the figgers we see about penitentiaries and things is got up the same way.

"Well, when I unhitched the horse and got him tended to and the potatoes covered up and all, I took the steak and started for the house. You know where I live—the barn is just back of the cottage, and there's a kind of little alley behind the barn and then the switch-yards come in; the railroad curves up toward the house after it passes the barn so it gets pretty near the kitchen. Of course, the trains bother us a good deal and the switch-engines are goin' back and forth all the time, and the house is pretty old and not very big, but all them things has to be taken into consideration in the rent, and I got it enough cheaper to make up. I presume that's the reason no poor people live out on the avenues, because the rents is so high, and in one way mebbe the switch-tracks is a good thing, for if it wa'n't for them I'd had to go out to the stock yards to live, and I'd rather have the engines and the smoke than the smell. Some of them Settlement people are tryin' to have a park made, out along the tracks right close to where we lived. Of course, flowers and grass would be nice, but I s'pose if they got the park some fellers would come along and pay more rent than we could afford and then we'd have to go out to the stock yards. It seems as if us poor people gets the worst of it no matter how you fix it. But I'm takin' an awful long while to get into the house; seems as if I'm tellin' you everything I've thought of ever since I've been locked up here in jail. It's mighty good of you to set and listen, and I'll always remember it as long as I live, though I guess that ain't sayin' much.

"When I come up to the door I heard the kid cryin' and she was scoldin' him about somethin' he'd done and tellin' him to go in the bedroom and stay till supper was ready and to quit his squallin' or she'd thrash him. Of course, generally, she was good to him, and I don't mean to say she wa'n't, but sometimes she got out of patience with him, same as all women does, I s'pose. Of course you have to make allowances for her. She dassent let the boy go to play back of the house, for there was the yards and the cars, and you know children always goes 'round cars; then she couldn't let him go in front for the electric road was there, and you know about that little boy bein' run over a year ago down at the corner. Then there's buildin's on both sides of us, so she had to have the kid right in the house all the time less'n she went out with him, and of course he got kind of tired settin' in the house all day with nothin' to do but look out in front and see the electric cars, or look out in the back and see the switch-engines. Still I sometimes thought she was crosser to him than she ought to have been at that.

"When I opened the door she was just takin' the boy into the bedroom. In a minute she come out and kind of slammed the door hard, and said, 'Well, you've got home, have you?' I said yes, I'd got home. That's every word I said. Then she said it was a pity that them drunken friends of mine couldn't keep me out all night spendin' the money for whiskey that I ought to use in the house. I told her that I hadn't spent no money for whiskey. She said 'Yes, your face looks it, and your breath smells it.' Then I told her that I did take one drink but the assessor bought it for me. Then she landed into the assessor, and told me I was in pretty company goin' 'round with him; that Mrs. McGinty had told her all about what kind of a man he was and she didn't want to hear any more about him. Then I asked her about when supper would be ready, and she said she hadn't begun to get it yet, that she'd been doin' the washin' and had that brat of mine to take care of all day, and she'd get the supper when she got ready. Of course I was hungry and cold, and that made me kind of mad, only I didn't say much, but laid the beefsteak on the table and unrolled it so's she could see it. I thought mebbe that would kind of tempt her, and I told her she'd better cook it and fry a few potatoes. She made some remark about the steak, and about how I'd better got a soup bone, or a chicken, or somethin' cheaper, and no wonder I was in debt with all the money I spent for whiskey, and when I did bring anything home to eat it had to be somethin' that cost a good deal more'n I could afford. Then I said that this was a rump steak and only cost fifteen cents, and she said I could get a soup bone that weighed six or seven pounds for that, and I hadn't any business to throw away my money. Then she kind of stopped for a few minutes and took the steak out into the kitchen. Where we'd been was in the settin' room. I went in to see the kid a few minutes and kind of quieted him down, and so long as he laid on the bed and seemed kind of like as if he'd go to sleep I shut the bedroom door and come out again. Then I picked up the paper and read about the alderman not goin' to run any more, and that was the real reason why he wa'n't goin' to give us any more turkeys; then I looked at the sportin' page and then I read a long story about a feller that had killed some one and left 'em dead in the house, and then run away, and how they'd found 'em dead and had offered a thousand dollars reward for the feller who killed the other one. Then I read about a murder trial that they was just havin' and how the jury had found the feller guilty and he was goin' to be hung, and how he never moved a muscle, and how his mother screamed and fell over in a swoond when the clerk read the verdict. While I was readin' she kept comin' out and in to the settin' room, bringin' dishes and things to set the table. You know we generally et in the settin' room. Ev'ry time she come in she kind of glared at me, but I let on not to notice her.

"Pretty soon I smelt the steak fryin' and went out in the kitchen. When I got out there I found the steak fryin' in the skillet all right and her just takin' up the tea kettle to pour water on it. Now this made me mad, for that wa'n't no way to fry steak. You know yourself that you lose all the flavor of the steak by pourin' water on it; that makes it more like boiled meat than it does like beefsteak. I just saw her in time, and I called out, 'What are you doin'? Put down that kettle. Don't you know any better'n to pour water on beefsteak?' She said, 'You shut up and go back in the settin' room, or I'll pour the water on you.' I said, 'No, you won't; put down that kettle. How many times have I told you better'n to pour water on steak? It's hard enough for me to get the money for a steak without lettin' you spoil it that way.' I started to grab her hand, but before I could reach it she tipped the nozzle over into the skillet and poured a lot of water in, and the steam and hot water and grease kind of spattered up in my face. I didn't know whether I struck her or not; anyhow I grabbed the kettle, and when the nozzle turned round some of the hot water got onto me, and burned me a little. I put the kettle down and said, 'Damn you, what do you mean by spoilin' the steak every time I get it? If you ever do a thing like that again, I'll cut your throat.'

"Now, of course, I hadn't no idea of cuttin' her throat, no matter how often she done it. 'Twas just a way I had of showin' how mad I was about what she'd done. You see she done it a-purpose for I'd told her plenty of times before, and I told her then before any of the water got into the skillet, and she just poured it in to spite me. Then she said 'You drunken loafer, I'd like to see you try to cut my throat. I just dare you to do it. You don't need to wait until you bring home another steak; 'taint likely I'll be here by the time you bring home any more steak. I don't care what the Settlement people and the priest says about it, I'm going to quit you. I've stood this thing just as long as I'm goin' to', and she fairly screamed, just on purpose, so the neighbors could hear.

"Now I didn't want them to know we was fightin', and I seen that she was so mad she couldn't control herself and didn't care who heard or what happened. The neighbors had come in once before, but they'd got pretty well used to our fights. But I thought it had gone about far enough and the steak couldn't be helped, so I went back into the settin' room and picked up the paper. In a few minutes she come in and says, 'Well, come, your old steak's ready, you've made so much fuss about it you'd better come and eat it and let it shut your mouth.' And she went on into the bedroom and got the kid. I drew up my chair and set down to the table. She put the kid into the high chair and then she set down on the other side. I cut up the steak and give each of 'em a piece with some fried potatoes, then we had some bread and butter and some tea. She poured out the tea and handed me a cup. There wa'n't any milk for the tea and I asked her why that was. She told me she didn't have any money to buy tickets, and if I wanted milk I'd better leave some money to buy tickets instead of spending it all for whiskey. I didn't make much of any answer to this but commenced eatin' my steak. Besides bein' boiled it was cooked almost to a crisp, and you couldn't hardly tell whether it was beefsteak or what it was; all the taste was out of it and gone into the water and the steam. I put some of the gravy on the potatoes; this was better'n the steak and tasted more like beef. I et up the potatoes and the steak and a few pieces of bread and butter, and cut up the kid's steak and showed him how to hold his knife so's to eat without cuttin' himself, and I didn't say a word to her and she didn't say a word to me. Of course, I could see by the way she looked that she was mad, and I presume she could see that I was, too; and probably both of us thought it was just as well not to say anything, 'specially so long as the kid was there. All the time I was eatin' I kept thinkin' about the way she'd poured the water into the steak and spoilt it, and how I'd been lookin' forward to it ever since I bought it on Thirty-fifth Street, and the more I thought of it the madder I got. If it had been the first time I don't think I'd have minded it near so much, but I'd told her about it ev'ry time I brought home a steak, and it seemed as if always we had a row pretty near as big as this, and every time she managed to pour the water into it and spoil it in spite of all that I could do. And this time it had been just the same thing again. Any one would have been mad if they'd been in my place; don't you think so yourself?

"Well, I finished my supper without sayin' a word to her, and she didn't say a word to me, and then I got up and went back into the settin' room and picked up the paper and commenced readin' again. In a minute she come along through with the kid and took him into the bedroom to put him to bed. After she'd been in there a while she came out and shut the door, and stood up for a minute lookin' over toward me. I thought she was waitin' for me to speak, so I just kept my eyes on the paper like as if I was readin', but I wa'n't. I hadn't cooled off a great deal since she poured the water on the steak, and could see that she hadn't neither, so I thought mebbe it was as well to have it out, but I was goin' to wait for her to begin. Of course, I hadn't no idea then of doin' anything like what I did. I was just mad and reckless and didn't care much, and would keep thinkin' of the steak, and you know all the time I was thinkin' I could feel a kind of prickin' up in my head, as if a lot of needles was runnin' up toward my hair. I s'pose it was the blood runnin' up there. That feller that I told you about that was talkin' to us over here kind of made out that a man was a good deal like a machine, or an engine of some kind, and when the steam was turned on he had to go. He said that if the blood was pumped up in the head it made us do things; it made some people write poetry, and some make speeches, and some sing, and some fight, and some kill folks, and they couldn't really help it if they was made that way and the blood got pumped up in the head. I believe there's a good deal in it. You know when the blood don't circulate down in your feet they get cold and kind of dead, and then if you put 'em into a pail of hot water or even cold water, and then rub 'em hard with a towel, they get prickly and red, and you can feel the blood comin' back to 'em and feel 'em wake up again.

"Well, I set perfectly still while she stood by

the mantel-piece. First she picked up one thing and then another and kind of dusted 'em and put 'em back. She done this till she had dusted ever'thing on the mantel-piece, and all the time she would be lookin' over toward me, but I kept my eyes down on the paper and pretended to be readin'. I knew that she didn't dust the things because she wanted to dust, for she always dusted in the mornin' just after she swept. I knew she did it because she was nervous and mad, and was waitin' for me to begin. Of course, sometimes when you are mad the longer you wait the more you get over it, and then sometimes the longer you wait the madder you get. It's like a boiler not usin' any of its steam while the fire is goin'; if it waits long enough somethin's got to happen.

"Finally after she got everything dusted she looked over straight at me and says 'Are you goin' to read that paper all night?' I told her I was if I wanted to, that it was none of her business how long I read it; there was a part of it that I'd like to give her to read if she wanted to; it was the cookery department, and had a recipe for frying steak. Of course, there wa'n't no such thing in the paper, and I just made it up and said it to be sassy, and I knew I shouldn't have been throwin' it up to her, but I was so mad I really didn't think how 'twould sound. Then she said she didn't want any advice from me or the paper either, about cookin', and she wanted me to understand that the cookin' was none of my business and she'd tend to that herself in her own way, and if ever I interfered again she'd leave me and take the kid with her. She said she learned cookin' long before she ever knew me. Then I said I thought she could make money by startin' a cookin' school; all them rich folks on Prairie Avenue would come over to get her to learn them how to fry steak. She said she guessed she knew more 'bout fryin' steak than I did, and when I boarded at the restaurant I was mighty glad to get steak fried that way, and I only grumbled about it now because I was so mean and didn't know how to treat a woman, and a man like me never had no right to have a decent wife. Then I said I wished I hadn't; I'd be a mighty sight better off by myself than livin' with her and havin' her spoil everything that came in the house, and I wished I was back boardin' in the restaurant where she found me. She said I didn't wish it half so much as she did, that she got along a good deal better when she was waitin' on the table than she had since she married me; then she had a chance to get out once in a while and see some one and have a good time, but now she stayed to home from one year's end to another lookin' after me and my brat. I told her I guessed the brat was just as much hers as it was mine, and I didn't think that was any way to speak about the boy. Of course I really knew that she didn't say it because she had anything against him, but just because she was mad at me. She always liked him, and I can't make any complaint of the way she treated him, and I want him to know it when we're both dead, and I don't want him to get any idea that she wa'n't perfectly square. I kind of want you to fix it, if you can, so 'twon't look to him as if either of us was to blame, but I guess that won't be an easy thing to do.

"Then I said she was mighty glad to give up the job she had at the restaurant to marry me. She said I asked her to get married, that she didn't ask me. Then I told her that, of course, she didn't ask me, but she gave me a mighty good chance, and that I believed she just got that red waist and fixed up her hair the way she did to ketch me, and when I spoke to her about marryin' it didn't take her very long to throw up her job, and take me so she could get supported without doin' anything. Then she said that if she spent any money to get that red waist to ketch me she was throwin' it away, and that if I thought she ever worked for any one else as hard as she did for me and my brat that I was mistaken, and it didn't make any difference what she done, I never gave her any thanks or did anything for her. If I ever had any time I spent it with them drunken loafers and politicians and never went anywhere with her; that she wa'n't no better'n a slave, and what was she doin' it all for; pretty soon she'd be old long before her time. Her looks was all gone now, and she hadn't even had a new dress for over a year. I told her that I didn't know what she wanted of looks, she never was a prize beauty and 'twant very like anybody'd ever be fool enough to marry her again, if anything happened to me. And she said if she ever got rid of me there wouldn't be much danger of her marryin' any one else, she had men enough to last as long as she lived; that all they ever thought of was what they could get to eat and drink, that I'd made more fuss over that miser'ble beefsteak than any one would over their soul, and she didn't see why she ever stood it from me, and she was just as good as I ever was and knew just as much, and worked a good deal harder, and didn't run 'round nights and get drunk and spend all the money with a lot of loafers, and be in debt all the time and have the collector runnin' after me. I told her I had just about enough of that kind of talk, and wouldn't stand no more of it from her; it was bad enough for her to burn up the beefsteak and spoil it without blackguardin' me and callin' me names; she was mighty glad to get the clothes and the grub I bought her and to live in my house and have me work hard every day in the cold to get money while she just stayed to home and played with the kid, and if she said another word to me I'd smash her face. Then she said, 'Yes, you miserable wife-beater, you kicked me once, didn't you, but you needn't think you can kick me or lay hands on me again. I ain't afraid of you nor any of your low-lived drunken crew!' Then she kind of reached back to the mantel and took hold of a plaster Paris lady I'd bought of a peddler, just as if she was goin' to throw it at me, same as she throwed that dish once before. I seen what she was doin' and I grabbed her arm and said, 'You damned bitch, don't try that on me'; and I gave her a kind of shove over toward a chair and she missed the chair and fell on the floor.

"Of course, you know I didn't really mean anything when I called her a damned bitch; that is, I didn't mean any such thing as any one might think from them words. You know us fellers down to the yards don't think very much about usin' that word, and we never really mean anything by it. But I don't think 'twas a very nice word to use and have always been sorry I said it, even if I did kill her.

"Well, she jumped up off'n the floor and made towards the table, like she'd grab a knife, and by this time I had a prickly feelin' runnin' all through my head and up into my hair, and I didn't really think of anything but just about her and what she was doin'. I don't believe I even thought about the kid in there on the bed. Mebbe if I had I wouldn't have done it.

"Well, when she made for the table that way, I just run over between her and the table, and said 'Damn you, if you move another step I'll knock your damned brains out!' Them's the very words I said. I didn't really think what I'd do, but of course I was mad and didn't mean to give up to her, and wanted to show her who was boss, and that's all I thought about. Then she come right up to me and sort of throwed her arms back behind her, and throwed her head back, and her hair hung down all kind of loose, and her eyes glared like electric lights, and she looked right at me and just yelled so I thought the people could hear her all over the ward. And she said, 'Kill me! you miserable drunken contemptible wife-beater; kill me, I just dare you to kill me! Kill me if you want to and then go in there and kill the boy, too; you'd better make a good job of it while you're at it! Kill me, you coward, why don't you kill me?'

"Just then I happened to look down by the stove and seen the coal pail, and there was the poker in the pail. The poker was long and heavy. Of course I hadn't ever thought anything about the poker, but I looked down there and seen it, and she kept yellin' right at me, 'Kill me! Kill me!' I said: 'Shut up your mouth, damn you, or I will kill you!' But she just yelled back, 'Why don't you do it! Kill me! Kill me! You miserable dirty coward! Kill me!' Then I looked down at the poker and I just reached and grabbed it, and swung back as hard as ever I could.

"Her face was kind of turned up toward me. I can see it now just as plain — I s'pose I'll see it when I'm standin' up there with the black cap over my eyes. She just leaned back and looked up as I swung my arm and she said: 'Kill me! Kill me!' And I brought it down just as hard as ever I could right over her forehead,— and she fell down on the floor."

V

"You might go and talk to the guard a little bit, I'll be all right in a few minutes. You know this is the first time I've ever told it, and I guess I'm a bit worked up."

Hank got up, without looking at Jim's face. His own was white as a corpse. He moved over to the little iron door and spoke to the guard.

"Could you give me a drink of water—or could you make it whiskey? I'm sure that would be better for Jim."

The guard passed him a flask, and told him to just keep it. Hank took a drink himself and handed it to Jim.

"Well, I guess 'twould do me good. I believe if I was out of here I wouldn't never take any more, but I don't see any use stoppin' now; anyhow I'll need a lot of it in the mornin'. Just ask the guard if any word has come for me. I s'pose he'd told me, though, if it had." Jim held the bottle to his mouth long enough to drink nearly half of what was left.

Hank looked out at the silent corridors. Over in the court he could still hear the hammer and the voices of the workmen; from the upper tiers, the wild shriek of an insane man called on some one to save him from an imaginary foe. A solitary carriage rolled along the pavement, and the voices of two or three men singing came up from the street below. A faint breath from the lake just stirred the heavy prison smell that seemed dense enough to be felt. The guard asked him how he was managing to pass the night. Hank answered that it was going much faster than he had thought.

"Poor fellow," said the guard, "I'll be kind of lonesome when he's gone. He's been a good prisoner." This was the highest character that a guard could give.

"Well, Hank, if you are ready now, I'll go on with my story. That whiskey kind of braced me up, and I s'pose you needed it too, after listenin' so long. I must hurry, for I ain't near through with what I wanted to say. I've thought lots about how I hit her, and I s'pose I ought to think it was awful, and it looks so to me now, and still it didn't seem so then. I can't help thinkin' of what that feller said to us in his speech. He claimed that punishin' people didn't do no good; that other people was just as likely to kill some one if you hung anybody, as they would be if you let 'em go, and he went on to say that they used to hang people for stealin' sheep and still just as many sheep got stole and probably more'n there was after they done away with it. I don't s'pose I ever should have thought anything about it if I hadn't killed her, but, of course, that made me think a lot. I'm sure that I wouldn't do such a thing again; I wouldn't be near so likely to do it as I was before, because now I know how them things commence, and I'm awful, awful sorry for her too. There wa'n't no reason why she should die, and why I should have killed her, and if there was anything I could do to change it, of course I would.

"But I can't really see how hangin' me is goin' to do any good. If it was I might feel different, but it ain't. Now, all my life I always read about all the murders in the newspapers and I read about all the trials and hangin's, and I always kind of wished I could go and see one. But I never thought I'd go this way. Why, I was readin' about a murder and how a feller was found guilty and sentenced to be hung just before I killed her. And do you s'pose I thought anything about it? If there'd been forty scaffolds right before my eyes I'd have brought down that poker just the same. I don't believe any one thinks of gettin' hung when they do it; even if they did think of it they'd plan some way to get 'round it when they made up their mind to do the killin'. But they don't think much about it. I believe sometimes that the hangin' makes more killin'. Now look at them car-barn fellers; they just went out and killed people regardless, same as some men go out to shoot game. I don't believe they'd 've done it if it hadn't been so dangerous. And then you know when they hung the whole three of 'em at once, and one feller cut his own throat so as to cheat 'em, and they took him right up and hung him, too, though he was so weak they had to carry him onto the scaffold, and the doctors done ever'-thing they could to keep him from dyin' just so's they could hang him. Well, you know they hadn't any more'n finished them until another gang of young fellers commenced doin' just the same kind of thing, and they are in jail now for murder, and you know one of 'em came in here one day and looked at the other ones before he done the killin'. I half believe that all the fuss they made 'bout them fellers and hangin' 'em and printin' it all in the newspapers did more to make the other ones do it than anything else. But I s'pose there ain't no use hangin' 'em unless you put it all in the newspapers, for it won't scare any one from doin' it unless people know they are hung.

"But, of course what I think about it don't make any difference, so I'd better hurry on. Well, after she fell over I stood still for a few minutes waitin' for her to get up. Of course I thought she'd get right up again, and mebbe come back at me. But she didn't move. Then I thought she was scarin' me, and I just sat down for a few minutes to show her that I wa'n't goin' to be fooled in no such way. Still she didn't stir. Then I commenced to be half scart and half mad. I didn't think it was right to try to make me believe I had done anything like that. So I said, 'When you've laid there long enough you'd better get up.' Then I said, 'What's the use of playin' theatre, you can't fool me. I'm goin' to bed and when you get ready you can come along.' But I didn't go to bed; I just sat still a little longer, and then I stepped over by her head and looked down at it, and I thought it didn't look right, and then I was scart in earnest. Just then I heard the kid cry, and I didn't want him to come out, so I locked the outside door and took a good look to see that all the curtains was clear down, and went in to see the kid. I lit a candle in the bedroom and talked with him a little; told him ever'thing was all right and to go to sleep, and I'd come in again in a minute or two. Then I went back to the settin' room to see her.

"Before I looked at her face I looked down to her feet to see if maybe they hadn't moved, for I didn't want to look at her face if I could help it. And I thought mebbe this would be the best way. But the feet was just where they was before; then I looked at her hands and they hadn't moved, so I knew I just had to look at her face. I hadn't examined her very close before, I was so scart, and I never could look at blood or dead folks, but of course this was different; so I got down on the floor close up to her face, and I seen the great welt along her forehead and top of her head and across the temple, and 'twas all covered with blood and a lot of it had got on the floor. Her eyes was wide open. I knew they didn't see anything. They looked just as if they'd been turned to glass, before she'd had time to shut 'em. I felt of her wrist to see if her pulse was goin'. At first I thought it wa'n't, and then I thought I felt it go a little, and I never felt so good in all my life. I pushed my finger down harder, but I couldn't get it again. Then I felt of her heart and it was just the same way. I leaned over to her ear, and asked her to please wake up, that I was awful sorry, and I didn't know what I was doin', and if she'd just speak I'd be good to her all my life and do ever'thing I could for her, and then I asked her to do it on account of the boy, but still she didn't move. Of course I was almost scart to death by this time; first I thought I'd call the neighbors and send for a doctor and then I thought that was no use. If she wa'n't dead I didn't need him, and if she was I must try to do somethin' so no one would find it out. Then I began to think what could be done to bring her to. I never had much experience with people that got hurt, except the ones I'd seen at the railroad, and I wa'n't just sure what to do with any one in this fix. But I'd read somethin' about it somewhere, and so I went into the back room and drew some water into a pail and took an old cloth and got down on the floor and commenced washin' her head. But I couldn't see the first sign of life. Then I looked around for some whiskey and found a little in a bottle in the closet and poured some in her mouth, but it all run right out, and she didn't move.

"Of course I never went to school very much but no matter how good an education I had I don't s'pose I could tell you how I felt so you'd know it yourself. I never s'posed I'd do anything to get into any trouble, and I always thought I was different from criminals. But here I was in the house with her dead, and I'd killed her, and what would happen to me? I just pictured the head-lines in the newspapers and the boys callin' 'all about the Jackson murder,' and me tried for murder and hung, and the kid goin' 'round the rest of his life knowin' that his father had killed his mother and then got hung.

"At first I just set paralyzed and sort of held my head in my hands and moaned, and wondered if mebbe it wa'n't a dream and if I couldn't wake up, and then I thought I'd go and give myself up to the police and be done with it, and then I thought I might just as well kill myself, so I went and got an old razor, that I used to shave with sometimes, and tried to get up my nerve to cut my throat. But somehow I couldn't put the edge over my wind-pipe. I wish though now that I had. Did you ever try to kill yourself? Them people that say it's only cowards that kill themselves don't know what they're talkin' about. I'd like to see them try it once. I'd have killed myself only I didn't have the nerve. It wa'n't because I cared anything about livin'; but I just couldn't cut my own throat. Then I thought mebbe she wa'n't dead, and I'd look again. So I done just the way I had before,—commenced at her feet to see if they'd moved, then when I got up to her hands I thought one of 'em had moved, and my heart just gave a great big jump. Then I remembered that I'd picked it up, when I'd felt for her pulse and had put it down in a different place. Then I looked up to her face and it was just the same. It was white as a sheet, all except the long red and black welt and the blood, and her eyes wide open, and lookin' right straight up to the ceilin' starin' just like a ghost. Then I felt of her hands and feet, and they was cold as ice and she was stiff, and I knew it was all off and she was dead.

"If you don't mind I'll just take a little more of that whiskey before I go on; the whole thing's been a little wearin' on me and I think it'll brace me up a bit. You'd better have some, too. That guard is a good feller, considerin' the place he's in. I believe if you hadn't come I'd told my story to him. I didn't feel as if I could go without tellin' some one how it really was. You see no one ever made the least bit of allowance for me in the trial, and I got tired of talkin' to my lawyer all the time. He always said that what I told him didn't amount to anything, and he was so well educated that he couldn't understand me anyhow.

"When I was sure that she was dead, I just

throwed myself over on the floor, and laid my face flat down on my arm and give up. I'm sure I cried and I thought they could hear me next door, but I guess they didn't. Anyhow I cried without payin' any attention to 'em. I must have laid this way for ten or fifteen minutes without once lookin' up, and she was right close to me, and I could just reach out my hand and touch her. And I hadn't begun to think what I'd do. Then after I'd laid a while, I just thought mebbe I'd ought to pray. It had been a long while since I'd prayed. Of course, I hadn't paid much attention to such things when I was all right; I guess there ain't many people that does, except women and children, but I always really believed in it, just the same as I do now. I kind of thought that God knew that I wasn't wicked enough to kill her, and have all this trouble, and bring all that misery on the kid; so I thought I'd try him. I didn't know much about prayers except only the ones I'd learnt long ago, and they didn't any of 'em seem to fit this case. But I didn't need to know any prayers; I just got down on my knees and prayed myself. I begged God to have her come back; I told him how good she was, and how the boy needed her and what a hard time I'd always had, same as I told you, only not near so long, and I apologized the best I could for not goin' to church more reg'lar and not ever prayin' to him, and I asked him to forgive me for the time I kicked her, and the other things I'd done, and I promised if he only would let her come back I'd always be good and take care of her and the boy, and never do anything wrong and always go to church and confessional, and love God and Jesus and the Virgin and all the saints, and quit politics and drinkin', and do right. I prayed and prayed, and I meant it all, too. And I don't believe it was all for myself, 'though I s'pose most of it was, but I really felt awful sorry for her, as I have ever since, and I felt awful sorry for the boy, who never had anything at all to do about it all.

"Then after I quit prayin' I got up slow, thinkin' that it might have done some good, and that mebbe she'd be all right, so I started in, just as I had before, with her feet to see if they'd moved. I s'pose the reason I done this way was that if I saw her head first and knew she was dead 'twould be all off the first thing; and when I commenced with her feet I always had some hope till I got clear up to her head. Well, her feet hadn't moved a bit. Then I went to her hands, and they was just in the same place, and I began to feel it wa'n't any use to look at her head; but I did. And there it was just as white as that plaster-Paris lady, and her eyes lookin' straight up.

"Then I felt sure 'twas all off. I'd done everything I could think of, and I'd prayed just as hard as I knew how, and I was sure no one ever meant it more'n I did or wanted it any more, and I knew, of course, God had seen the whole thing and could do it if he wanted to and that he didn't want to, and that she was clear dead. I kind of half set and half laid down on the floor a little while longer, tryin' to think about it and what I was goin' to do. But I couldn't make any plans; I kep' thinkin' about how it had all happened, and it begun to seem as if it wa'n't really me that hit her with the poker, but as if both of us was somebody else and I was sort of dreamin' about it all. Ain't you ever had them kind of feelin's when somethin' awful has happened? But, of course, nothin' like that ever happened to you. I thought most about that beefsteak, and how I stopped and bought it, and didn't go in and get a drink, and all the time it seemed to me just as if that was where I made my big mistake. And then I thought how awful near I come to goin' into the saloon instead of the butcher-shop, and then some of the time I'd kind of feel as if mebbe

I was goin' into the saloon after all, and it wa'n't goin' to happen. Don't you know how it is when anybody's died or anything happened? You think about everything that's done, so as to see if mebbe you can't make it come out some other way after all? Well, that's the way I done about every little thing, and every word we both spoke till I hit her with the poker. Another thing where I almost missed killin' her was that poker; that coal pail didn't belong in the settin' room at all, but ought to have been in the kitchen, and I don't know how it ever got in there. Mebbe the boy lugged it in for a drum. You know he didn't have many playthings, or mebbe she started a little fire in the settin' room, for 'twas the first cold day. I don't see how it could have been that either, for she was washin' that day and wouldn't have any time to set in there. But I don't know as it makes any difference; the coal pail was in the settin' room and the poker was in the pail, and they was right before my eyes at the time. If they hadn't been I never would've used the poker. When she stood up and told me to kill her, I'd most likely struck her with my fists and that would only knocked her down. But anyhow it didn't do any good to go over it, for I couldn't go into the saloon instead of the butcher-shop, and I couldn't get that coal pail out of the settin' room, and it had all been done—and she was dead! And I'd killed her! After I'd went over this a long time I made myself stop so I could do somethin' that would be some use, for I knew there was lots to be done before mornin', and I hadn't a minute to lose. I knew I must get up off'n the floor and try to act like a man, and not give up, no matter how bad it was. But before I got up I thought I'd just take one more look to make sure that there wa'n't no use. So I went over her again, just as I'd done before, and it came out the same way anyhow. I didn't much think it was any use then and would've just about as soon begun at the head and got through with it right away.

"After I had looked her over again I got up and set down in a chair to make up my mind what to do. I hadn't been there very long when I knew I couldn't figure it out; 'twas too much for me the way I was, and so I thought I'd just quit tryin' and do a few things first. And then I wondered what time 'twas. I hadn't thought anything about the time before, but I s'posed it must be almost mornin' for just then I heard an express wagon drive along the street, and anyhow it seemed an awful long while since I got home. The clock was right up on the mantel piece and tickin' loud, but I hadn't thought of lookin' at it before and didn't even know it was in the room. I looked up and seen it was goin' and that 'twas only a quarter to twelve. I was surprised that it wa'n't no later, and wondered how it could be, and just then it struck and I kind of kep' count because I was sort of thinkin' of the clock and it stopped strikin' at nine. Then I thought somethin' must be wrong with the clock too, and I looked back again and seen that I'd made a mistake in the hands and 'twas only nine o'clock. I couldn't believe this was so, but the clock was goin' all right. Then I kind of braced up a little and thought what was to be done. First, I looked 'round the room. I told you, didn't I, that we et in the settin' room? It was a settin' room and a dinin' room both. Sometimes we et in the kitchen, but that was pretty small. The table stood there with the dirty dishes just as we'd got through eatin'. There was the plates and knives and forks, and the tea-cups and the big platter with some of that steak left, and the gravy gettin' kind of hard like lard all 'round it. The coal pail was there and the poker down on the floor. The chairs was standin' 'round the table where we'd set to eat, except the rockin' chair which was over by the stove. I looked at all them things, and then I looked down at the floor, and there she lay with her head over toward the closet door and her feet up almost under the table. It was an awful sight to look at her on the floor, but there wa'n't nothin' else to do, so I looked her all over as careful as I had before, then I got kind of scart; I hadn't never been in a room alone with any one that was dead, except at the morgue; but, of course, this was worse than anything of that kind. I'd always heard more or less about ghosts and haunted houses and things like that, and didn't believe anything of the kind, but they seemed to come back now when I looked over where she was layin'. I was afraid of ever'thing, not of people but of ghosts and things I couldn't tell nothin' about. I knew she was dead and must have gone somewhere, and most likely she was right 'round here either in the bedroom lookin' at the boy or out here seein' how I felt and what I was goin' to do with her. Just then I heard somethin' move over by the closet and it scart me almost to death. I knew it must be her and couldn't bear to see her unless she could come to life down on the floor. Finally I looked around to where I heard the noise and then I seen it was the curtain; the window was down a little at the top. I went and put up the window, and then hated to turn 'round and look back where she lay. Then I went to the bedroom door and opened it about half way just so the light wouldn't fall on the bed and wake him up, but so I could hear him breathe and it wouldn't be quite so lonesome. Ever'thing was awful still and like a ghost except the clock, after I got to thinkin' of it. Then it ticked so loud I was almost 'fraid they'd hear it in the next house. When I got the bedroom door open I thought I must do somethin' about her and the room before I made up my mind what plan to take about myself.

"First I went and hunted up the cat. I'd always heard about that, so I went into the kitchen and there she was sleepin' under the stove. I couldn't help wishin' I was the cat, although I had never thought of any such thing before. Then I took her in my hand and went to the outside door and threw her out in the yard and shut the door tight. Then I came back in the settin' room and thought about what had to be done. I looked over again at her and then I saw her eyes still lookin' right up at the ceilin', and round and shinin' like glass marbles. I thought that wa'n't the way they ought to be and that all the dead folks I'd ever seen had their eyes shut. So I went over and got down by her head and kind of pushed the lids over her eyes, same as I'd always heard they did, and put some nickels on 'em to keep 'em down. I don't know how I done it, but I felt as if it had to be done, and, of course, they wa'n't no one else to do it, and nobody knows what they can do until they have to. And then I saw that there was a good deal of blood on her face, and I wanted her to look decent though I didn't know then what would be done with her, and I went into the kitchen to the sink and got a pan of water and some soap and an old towel, and washed all the blood off that I could find, and wiped her face careful to make her look as well as I could. One or twice while I was doin' it I kind of felt down to her heart, but I knew it wa'n't no use. Still I thought it couldn't do any hurt, and that God might've thought I wa'n't scart enough so he waited; but I didn't feel nothin' there. Then I kind of smoothed back her hair like I'd seen her do sometimes. 'Twas all scattered round on the floor and pretty full of blood. I couldn't very well get the blood out, but I fixed the hair all back together the best I could. Then I noticed that her jaw kind of hung down and I pushed it up and tied a towel around it to keep it there, and then she looked pretty well, except that great long gash over her face and head where the poker went.

"Then I thought I'd have to fix up the room and the floor a little bit. I sort of pushed back the chairs and the table so I could get a little more room, and then moved her a little way and straightened her out some. First before I moved her I got that paper I'd been readin' and laid it on the floor and then I took up her shoulders and lifted 'em over to one side and laid her head on the paper. Then I moved the rest of her over to match her head and shoulders. There was a lot of blood on the floor where she'd been, and I knew I had to do somethin' about that.

"There was a nice Japanese rug on the floor, and her head had struck just on the edge of it over by the door. I'd bought her the rug for a Christmas present last year, and she liked it better'n anything she had in the house, but it was beginnin' to wear out some. A part of the blood was on the floor and a part on the rug. So I went and got another pan of water and the soap and towel and washed the floor; then I washed the rug the best I could, and lifted it up and washed in under it, and then threw away the water and got some more and washed it all over again. When I seen that the last water was a little bloody I thought mebbe I'd better go over it again, so I got some more water and went over it the third time, then I threw the water out and washed the towel as good as I could, and went back in and looked 'round the room to see if there was anything else to do. Just then I noticed the poker that I hadn't thought of before. I took it to the kitchen and washed it all over and then dried it and then put it in the stove and covered it with ashes, and then laid it down on the hearth; then I went back in and seen that ever'thing was finished and that she was all right, and there wa'n't nothin' to do except to make my plans. But before I go on and tell you what I done with her, let me speak to the guard a minute."

Hank and Jim got up once more and looked out through the bars. The guard was still sitting on the stool and asked what he could do.

"What time is it?" said Jim.

"Oh, it's early yet, only a little after twelve," he replied. "Wouldn't you like a little more whiskey? I've got another bottle here, and I can get all I want down to the office. If I was you I'd drink it. I don't think whiskey does any hurt. I'm always arguing with that other guard about it. He's bug-house on whiskey."

Jim took the whiskey and then turning to the guard, with an anxious face, said "You're sure nothin' has come for me?"

"No, there's nothin' come." But after a few minutes he added, "I'll go over to the telephone pretty soon and call up the telegraph office and make sure."

Jim's face brightened a little at this. "I'm much obliged. It might be sent to me, and it might be sent to the jailer or the sheriff. You'd better ask for all of us."

VI

"That whiskey makes me feel better. I've been takin' a good deal to-night and I s'pose I'll take more in the mornin'. That's one reason why I'm drinkin' so much now. First I thought I wouldn't take any to-morrow — or — I guess it's to-day, ain't it? It don't seem possible; but I s'pose it is. I thought I'd show the newspapers and people that's been tellin' what a coward I was to kill a woman; but now I think I'll take all I possibly can. I guess that's the best way. It don't make no difference — if I take it they'll say I'm a coward and if I don't, it's only bravado. Most people takes so much that they almost have to be carried up, and they don't hardly know. I guess that's the best way. Some people take somethin' to have a tooth pulled, and I don't see why they shouldn't for a thing like this. Mebbe the whiskey makes me talk more'n I meant to, and tell you a lot of things that hain't nothin' to do with the case, but it's pretty hard for me to tell what has and what hain't.

"After I got her all laid out and the floor cleaned,

I set down a minute to think what I'd do next. First I thought I'd go in and get the kid and take him away, and leave her there, and I guess now that would have been the best way, and they wouldn't found it out so quick. But then I thought the people next door, or the postman, or milkman, or somebody, would come along in the mornin' and find her there, and I couldn't get far with the kid. Besides I only had about ten dollars and I knew that wouldn't last long. Then I thought I'd just go out and jump onto one of the freight-trains they was makin' up in the yards, and leave her and the kid both; then I couldn't bear to think of him wakin' up and comin' out into the settin' room and findin' her there. He wouldn't know what it meant and would be scart to death and 'twouldn't be right. Then so long as I couldn't do either one, I had to get her out, but I didn't know how to do it, and what was I goin' to do with her when I got her out. First I thought I'd try to put her in the sewer, and then I knew some one would find her there for that had been tried before; then I studied to see what else I could think of.

"Finally I happened to remember a place she and I went once picnicin', just after we was married. I don't know how I happened to remember it, 'cept that I couldn't think of anything to do, and then I was kind of goin' over our life, and it seemed as if that was the nicest day we ever had. One of the boys had been tellin' me about the new street car lines that run way off down through Pullman and South Chicago, and out into the country, and how nice it was out there away from all the houses. So one Sunday we went over to the street cars and started out. I don't know whether we found the right place or not, but I remember just when we was goin' to turn somewhere to go to Pullman or South Chicago we saw some trees off in a field, and thought that would be a nice place to go and set in the shade and eat the lunch we'd brought along. So we went over under the trees, and then I saw some rocks further over, and then she and I went over where they was and there was a great deep pond with big stones all 'round the edge. I heard that it was an old stone quarry that had got filled up with water. But it was awful deep and big, and we set down under a little tree on top of one of them big rocks and let our feet hang over the sides, and the water was way down below, and I said to her just in fun, 'Now, if I wanted to get rid of you, I could just push you over here and no one would ever know anything about it.' She kind of laughed at the idea and said if I ever wanted to get rid of her I wouldn't have to push her off any rock, that she'd go and jump in somewhere herself, and I told her if I ever wanted her to I'd let her know, and for her to just wait till I did. And we went all 'round the pond, and I threw stones in it and tried to see how near across I could throw, and we stayed 'round until it was time to take the car and go home. And I don't believe I ever had a better time. Now and then when we was friendly or had got over a fight, we used to talk about goin' back there again, but we never did.

"Well, after thinkin' of ever'thing I could, I made up my mind that the best thing was for me to put her on the express wagon and take her out there, if I could find the place. I didn't believe anybody would ever know anything about it, and if they did 'twould be a long time and they wouldn't know who she was.

"Then I thought it might be dangerous gettin' her out of the house and gettin' the wagon out on the street that time of night. If any one seen us they'd be suspicious and want to know what I was doin', and then I was afraid the policeman would be watchin' for suspicious people and things along the street. But I didn't see anything else to do, and I knew I had to take chances anyway and would most likely get caught in the end. I looked at the clock and found 'twas only ten, and I felt as if that was too early to start out. The people next door wouldn't be abed and if they ever saw me carryin' her out they couldn't help noticin' it. So I set down and waited. You hain't no idea how slow the time goes in such a case. I just set and heard that clock tick, and the boy breathin' in the other room; it seemed as if every tick was just fetchin' me that much nearer to the end—and I s'pose mebbe that's so, whether we've killed anyone or not, but you don't never think of it unless it's some place where you're waitin' for someone to die, or somethin' like that. Then of course I kept thinkin' of ever'thing in my whole life, and I went over again how I'd done it, but I couldn't make it come out any different no matter how hard I tried.

"Then I wondered what I was goin' to do next, and how long 'twould be before they'd ketch me, and if I'd stand any show to get out, if I got ketched. Of course, I thought I'd have to run away. I never seemed to think of anything but that. I guess ever'body runs away when they do any such thing; 'tain't so much bein' safer, but they want to get away. It don't seem as if they'd ever be any chance any more where it's done. But I couldn't just figger out where to go. Of course, I knew I'd take the cars. There ain't any other way to travel if you want to go quick. Then I thought I'd have a long enough time to figger it out while I was takin' that drive down across the prairie. Anyhow I'd need somethin' to think about while I was goin'.

"That feller that talked to us in the jail said the real reason why they hung people and locked 'em up was to get even with 'em, to make 'em suffer because they'd done somethin'. He said all the smart men who'd studied books claimed that hangin' and punishin' didn't keep other people from doin' things. But if it's done to make anyone suffer they ain't any use in doin' it at all. I never suffered so much since as I did when I was settin' there and thinkin' all about it, and what I was goin' to do, and what would become of the kid, and how she was dead, and ever'thing else. You know it takes quite a while to get used to a thing like that, and while I was settin' there beginnin' to realize what it all meant, it was awful! If I'd only had the nerve I'd just cut my throat and fell right over alongside of her. A good many people does that and I wish I could 've. But every time I thought of it I kind of hung back. I don't ever want any more such nights; I'd rather they'd hang me and be done with it. I didn't suffer so much when I was runnin' away or gettin' caught, or bein' tried; even when I was waitin' for the verdict to come in; nor I didn't suffer so much waitin' for the Supreme Court or the Governor, or even since they give up hope and I can hear 'em puttin' that thing up over there in the court-yard.

"I don't s'pose hangin' will hurt so very much after all. The main thing is, I want 'em to hurry after they start out. Of course, I'll be pretty drunk, and won't know much about what they're doin', and I don't s'pose they'll take long after I put on them clothes until it's all over. Goin' from here to the place won't hurt, though I s'pose it'll be pretty hard work walkin' up the ladder and seein' that rope hangin' over the beam, and knowin' what it's for. But I s'pose they'll help me up. And then strappin' my hands and feet'll take some time. But they don't need to do that with me for I shan't do a thing;—still mebbe if they didn't I'd kind of grab at the rope when they knocked the door out from under my feet.

I might do that without knowin' it. So I s'pose it's just as well. It must be kind of sickish when they tie the rope 'round your neck, and when they pull that cap over your head, and you know you ain't never goin' to see anything again. I don't s'pose they'll wait long after that; they oughtn't to. You won't feel anything when you're fallin' down through, but it must hurt when you're pulled up short by the neck. But that can't last long, can it? They do say the fellers kicks a good deal after they're hung, but the doctors say they don't really feel it, and I s'pose they know, but I don't see how they can all be so smart about ever'thing; they hain't never been hung.

"I s'pose the priest will be here; he's a trump, and I think more of him than I ever did before. He's been a great help to me, and I don't know what I'd done without him. Of course, he talks religion to me, but he's kind of cheerful and ain't always making out that I'm so much worse than anyone else ever was. I ain't much afraid 'bout God; somehow I kind of feel as if He knows that I've always had a pretty tough time, and that He'll make allowances on account of a lot of them things that the judge ruled out, and He knows how I've suffered about it all and how sorry I be for her and the kid, and He'll give me a fair show. Still sometimes I can't help wonderin' if mebbe there ain't nothin' in all of it, and if I hain't got through when my wind's shut off. Well, 'scuse me, I didn't want to make you feel bad, but I've thought about it so much and gone over it so many times that it don't seem as if it was me, but that some one else was goin' to get hung; but I hain't no right to tell it to anybody else, and I didn't mean to.

"Well, I set there and waited and waited, until about eleven o'clock, and then I thought mebbe 'twould be safe enough to start. Just then the boy woke up, and I heard him say 'Mamma', and it kind of gave me a start, and I hurried in and asked him what he wanted and he said he wanted a drink of water, and I came out to the kitchen sink and got it and took it back and gave it to him. Then he asked me what time it was, and I told him about eleven o'clock, and he asked me why I had my clothes on and where mamma was, and I told him we hadn't gone to bed yet, and for him to turn over and go to sleep, and he said a few more words and then dropped off.

"Then I went out to the barn to hitch up the rig. The horse was layin' down asleep, and I felt kind of mean to wake him, for I knew he was about played out anyhow; but it couldn't be helped, so I got him up and put on the harness. I s'pose he didn't know much about the time, and thought he was goin' down to Water Street after a load of potatoes. I didn't bring any lantern; I knew the barn so well I could hitch up in the dark. Then I took the hay off'n the potatoes and put it in the bottom of the wagon to lay her on, and then run the wagon out and turned it 'round and backed it in again. I 'most always hitched up outside the barn for there was more room outdoors, but I didn't want to be out there any more'n I could help, so I thought I'd get all ready in the barn so I could just drive away.

"Well, I got the horse all harnessed and the bits in his mouth, and ever'thing ready to hitch up, and then went back in the house. I'd been thinkin' that I'd better take one more look, not that 'twould do any good but just because it might. You know when you've lost a knife, or a quarter, or anything, and you look through all your pockets and find it 'tain't there, and then go back and look through all of 'em again and don't find it; then you ain't satisfied with that and mebbe you keep a lookin' through 'em all day, even when you know 'tain't there. Well, that's the way I felt about her, only I s'pose a good deal worse, so when I got in I looked her over again just the same way's I had before. I felt for her pulse and her heart but 'twa'n't no use. Then I got my old overcoat and my hat and got ready to start, but before I left I thought I'd just look out once to see if the folks in the next house was abed, and I found they wa'n't, for there was a light in the kitchen right next to mine, and I knew 'twould never do to carry that kind of a bundle out the back door while they was up. So I waited a little while until the light went out and ever'thing was still, and then put on my coat and hat and picked her up in my arms. It was an awful hard thing to do, but there wa'n't nothin' else for it, so I just kind of took my mind off'n it and picked her up. When I got her kind of in my arms one of her arms sort of fell over, and her legs kind of hung down like they was wood, and then I see I had to fasten 'em some way or I couldn't never carry her. It wa'n't like a live person that can stay right where they want to; it was more like carryin' an arm full of wood that would scatter all around unless you get it held tight.

"Then I laid her down and found some string and tied her arms tight around her body, and then fastened her ankles together. Then I went into the bedroom and got a quilt off'n our bed and rolled her up in that. You know at my trial they made out that 'twas bad for me to tie her that way, and if I hadn't been awful wicked I wouldn't have done it. But I can't see anything in that; there wa'n't no other way to do it. Then they said it was awful bad the way I took her off and the place I dumped her, and the newspapers made that out one of the worst things about it all; but I tried to think up something else to do and I couldn't, and there she was dead, and I had to do the best I could. I washed her and fixed her all up before I went away, and if there'd been anything else I could have done I know I would.

"When I got her fixed up, I went to the door and looked out, and I saw some drunken fellers goin' along in the alley, so I waited a minute for them; and then I got her in my arms and opened the door and then turned off the light and went out and shut the door as soft as I could. It wa'n't but a few steps to the barn, but I hurried as fast as I could, and just as I was takin' the first step I heard the most unearthly screech that scart me so I 'most dropped her; but in a minute I knew it was only a train pullin' into the yards and I hurried to get to the barn before the engine come up.

"Well, I guess nobody saw me, and I got her in the wagon and laid her on the hay. I fixed her head to the end and her feet reachin' up under the seat. I didn't want her head so near me in that long drive down over the prairie. Then I covered her up the best I could with one of the old horse blankets, so it wouldn't look suspicious if any one seen me.

"I tell you it was awful pokerish out there in the barn, worse than in the house, for I had a light there. I didn't want to stay in the barn a minute longer than I could help, so I hurried and hitched the old horse onto the wagon, then went out to the alley and looked up and down to see if any one was there. Then I got on the seat and put a blanket around me and drove off. I was afraid the neighbors would notice me drive out of the barn, but they didn't. The moon hadn't quite got up and there couldn't any one see unless they was right close. When I got about a block away I seen a policeman walkin' 'long the street and goin' up to pull a box. Of course I was scart; he looked at me kind of suspicious like, and looked at the wagon to see what was in there, but it was rather dark and I braced up the best I could and drove right 'long and he didn't say nothin'. Then I found a lot of fellers that was comin' down the street makin' a lot of noise. They was a gang of politicians that had been goin' round to the saloons and was pretty full. I was afraid some of 'em might know me, but they didn't pay any attention and I went along up to the corner of Halsted and turned south. I knew Halsted was a pretty public street, but the roads was better and I had a long way to go, so I thought I might just as well chance that.

"I got along down about Twenty-ninth Street and met a gang of fellers that was makin' a lot of noise singin' and talkin', and braggin' and tellin' what they could do. I was a little 'fraid of 'em, not because I thought they'd hurt me, but I didn't know but what they'd see what was in the wagon. When I come up to 'em they told me to stop, that they was the "Bridgeport threshers" and no one had any right there but them, and they wanted to know what reason I had to be out at that time o' night. I told 'em I was just gettin' home, that I'd been kep' late up town. Then one of em' said, 'What you got in the wagon?' and I said 'Potatoes.' Then one feller said, 'Let's see 'em,' and started for the wagon. But another one spoke up and said 'Oh, Bill, leave him alone, he's all right.' And then they all started up another road and went away. That was a pretty narrow escape and I was 'most scart to death for fear they'd look under the blanket. I met a good many teams but nothin' more happened till I got down to Fifty-fifth Street Boulevard, where I turned east to go over to the Vincennes road.

"By this time the moon had come up and it was about as light as day. It had stopped snowin' and the wind had gone down but it was awful cold. I never saw a nicer night. You could see everything almost as well as daylight. I hurried the old horse as much as I could, but he couldn't go fast. He hadn't got much rested from the day before. Every once in a while I looked back at the load. I kind of hated to look, but I couldn't help it. The blanket commenced to kind of take her shape so it looked to me as if any one would know that some one was under there. So I got out and moved the blanket and fixed it up more on one side. But I didn't look at her. Then I drove on across to Vincennes road and turned south. Every once in a while I'd meet some one, and I was afraid all the time that something would happen, but it didn't and

I drove on. The moon got clear up high and I could see everything on the road and around the wagon, and see where her feet came through under the seat and almost touched mine, and could see all the horse blanket that covered her up. I hadn't got far down the Vincennes road until I thought the blanket had changed its shape and was lookin' just like her again so I got out and fixed it up and went back and drove on.

"While I was goin' 'long I kep' thinkin' what I was goin' to do and I s'pose it was the cold that made me think I'd better go south. I always did hate cold weather, and this winter I thought I'd have to stay out and run 'round from one place to another, if I didn't get caught the first thing.

"Then I thought I must take the horse and wagon back home, and I wanted to see that the boy was all right; so I thought it might bother me to go clear out to that quarry and get away from Chicago before daylight. But anyhow I could go until one o'clock and then get back by three, and probably ketch a train before mornin'.

"After a while I begun to have a queer idea about her. I thought I could feel her lookin' right at me,—kind of feel her eyes. I drove on, and said it was all bosh and she couldn't do it, and I looked down at her feet and I seen they was in the same place, but still I couldn't get over that feelin'. I thought she was lookin' at me all the time, and I kind of 'magined I could hear her say, 'Where 're you takin' me? Where are you takin' me? Where are you takin' me? just about the same as when she said, 'Kill me! Kill me! Kill me!' and no matter what I done, or how hard I tried, I could feel her lookin' and hear them words in my ears.

"By this time I was gettin' way down the Vincennes road. You know it gets wide way down south, and it ain't much built up nor very well paved. There's a lot of road-houses along the street; most of 'em was open and a good many fellers was 'round 'em, just as they always is 'round saloons. I'd like to have had a drink, for I was awful cold and scart, but I didn't dare go in, though I did stop at a waterin'-trough in front of one of the places and watered the horse. He was pretty well blowed and was hot. I had urged him pretty hard and the road was heavy. Wherever there was mud it was frozen so stiff that it could almost hold up, and still let you break through, the very worst kind of roads for a horse to go on.

"After I got him watered I went on and kep'

meetin' lots of wagons. I never had no idea how many people traveled nights before. I s'posed I wouldn't see any one, but I met a wagon ever' little ways and I was always afraid when I passed 'em. A great many of 'em hollered out, 'Hello, pardner,' or 'What you got to sell,' or anything, to be sociable, and I would holler back the best I could, generally stickin' to 'Potatoes,' when they asked me about my load. I thought I knew potatoes better'n anything else, and would be more at home with 'em if anything was said.

"I hadn't got far after I watered the horse before her eyes began to bother me again. Then I kept hearin' them words plainer than I had before. Then I got to thinkin' about all the things I had heard and read about people who were dead, and about murders, and that seemed to make it worse'n ever. Then I began to think of the things I'd read about people that were put away for dead, when they wa'n't dead at all, and about mesmerism, and hypnotism, and Christian science, but I knew none of them things was done the way she'd been killed. Then I remembered about trances, and how people was give up for dead sometimes for days, and even buried and then come to life, and about how people had dug up old graveyards and found out where lots of people had moved around after they's dead. And then I thought I heard her say, 'You thought you'd killed me! You thought you'd killed me! You thought you'd killed me!' And the further I went the plainer it sounded. Finally I began to think 'twas so and of course I hoped it was, and I kep' thinkin' it more'n more and couldn't get it out of my head. Of course, I looked around at the houses and the trees and fences and at the moon. It had clouded up a little with them kind of lightish heavy clouds you've seen that run so fast; they was just flyin' along over the sky and across the moon, and I was wishin' I could go 'long with 'em and get away from it all, and then the voice would come back, 'Where are you takin' me? Where are you takin' me? Where are you takin' me? You thought you'd killed me! You thought you'd killed me! You thought you'd killed me!' And I felt so sure she wa'n't dead that I couldn't stand it any more, and I looked at her feet, but they hadn't moved, and then I stopped the horse and got off'n the wagon and went back to the hind end and lifted up the blanket kind of slow. For I felt as if I'd stand more chance that way than if I did it all at once, and I got the blanket up, and then I got hold of the quilt just by the edge and kind of pulled it back so as to uncover her face, and just then the moon came out from behind a cloud and shone right down in her face, almost like day, and she looked just as white as a ghost, and the bandage had come off her jaw and it hung clear down, and her mouth was open, and I knew she was dead.

"Then I threw the things back and jumped onto the wagon, half crazy, and hurried on.

"It was gettin' now where there wa'n't no more houses, and I hardly ever met any teams, and I was gettin' clear out on the prairies, and I looked at my old silver watch and saw it was close to one o'clock, and I thought mebbe I might just as well get through with it now as to wait any longer. So I looked along at the fields to find a good place, and after a while I saw where there was a great big field full of hummocks. It looked as if they'd been diggin' for gravel or somethin' of that kind, and I thought that was as good a place as any. So I looked up and down the road, and saw no one comin', and I drove the old horse up in the fence corner and got off the wagon, and then I fixed a good place to get over, and fastened the quilt a little better, and took her in my arms and started as fast as ever

I could. I went past the fence and run over to the first hummock, but the hole didn't look very deep, and there was some more further over. So I went to them, but they wa'n't deep enough either. Then I looked 'round and saw one bigger'n the rest and went there. I laid her down and looked over. The moon was shinin' all right, and I could see that the hole was pretty big and deep. I laid her down lengthwise 'long the bank, and then took one more feel of her heart and 'twas just the same. Then I fastened the quilt a little tighter, lifted her clear over to the edge, and held her head and feet in a straight line so she'd roll down the hill all right, and then I give her a shove and turned and run away."

VII

"WELL, I hadn't any more'n started to run till I heard a splash and I knew she'd got to the water all right and there wa'n't nothin' for me to do but hurry home.

"I went right back to the wagon and climbed up on the seat and turned 'round. The old horse was pretty tired but he seemed some encouraged, bein' as he'd turned home. Horses always does, no matter how poor a place they has to stay. I urged him 'long just as fast as I could; didn't stop for nothin' except to give him some water at a trough down on Halstead Street, and went right home. Then I put him in the stable and took care of him, and throwed some hay in the manger. So long as I hadn't any oats I emptied about a bushel of potatoes in with the hay. I thought they wouldn't be any use to me any more, and they'd keep him quiet a while and mebbe do him some good.

"Then I went in the house, and struck a match and lit the lamp. I didn't 'low to stay long for I'd got my plans all thought out comin' home, but I just wanted to look into the room and see the kid. I glanced 'round and ever'thing seemed all right, except I thought I'd better take the coal pail out in the kitchen. Then I looked at the floor and the rug and I couldn't see no blood; and the water had pretty near dried up. Then I opened the bedroom door and looked at the kid. He was sleepin' all right, just as if he hadn't been awake once all night. He was layin' on one side with his face lookin' out toward me, and was kind of smilin' pleasant-like and his hair was all sweaty and curly. You've seen the kid. You know he's got white curly hair just as fine as silk. That's one thing he got from her.

"Well, I couldn't hardly bear to go away and leave him, but there wa'n't nothin' else to do. I guess I would have kissed him if I hadn't been 'fraid he'd wake up, but I never was much for kissin'; kissin' depen's a good deal on how you're raised. I guess rich people kiss a good deal more'n poor people, as a general rule, but I don't know as they think any more of their childern. Well, I just looked at him a minute and shut the door and went out. Then I noticed the whiskey-bottle on the table that I brought out to try to wake her; I hadn't thought of it before; and I picked it up and drank what was left, and turned and blew out the lamp and went away.

That's the last I ever seen of the kid, or the house.

"I went right over to the yards to see about trains. There wa'n't nothin' standin' 'round there and I didn't like to ask any questions, so I went down to the other end and see 'em switchin' some cars as if they was makin' up a train, and I walked out in the shadow of a fence until they'd got it all made up and I felt pretty sure 'twas goin' south. I knew them cars and engines pretty well. Then I jumped in a box car that was about in the middle of the train. There was a great big machine of some kind in the car, so there was plenty of room left for me, and I snuggled down in one corner and dozed off. I don't think I'd been sleepin' long till a brakeman come past with a lantern and asked me who I was and where I was goin'. I told him I was goin' south to get a job, and wanted to get down as far as Georgia if I could, for my lungs wa'n't strong and the doctors had advised a change of climate. I had read about the doctors advisin' rich people to have a change of climate, but of course I hadn't ever heard of their tellin' the poor to do any such thing. I s'pose because it wouldn't do no good and they couldn't afford to leave their jobs and go. But I didn't see why that wasn't a good excuse. He asked me if I had any whiskey or tobacco, and I said no, and he told me that I oughtn't to get on a train without whiskey or tobacco, and I promised not to again, and then he let me go.

"It was just gettin' streaks of light in the east, and I thought I might as well go ahead and prob'-bly I'd better ride till noon anyhow, as nothin' much could happen before that time. Then I went off to sleep again. The sun was pretty high before I woke up. I looked at my watch to see what time it was but found I'd forgot to wind it the night before and it had run down. Well, I concluded it was just as safe to stay on the car so long as it was goin' south and so I didn't get off all day, except to run over to a grocery when the train stopped once and get some crackers and a few cigars. I thought I'd have 'em when the brakeman come 'round, and then I fixed my-self for the night. I was pretty well beat out and didn't have much trouble goin' to sleep, though of course I couldn't get it out of my head any of the time, and would wake up once in a while and wonder if it wa'n't all a dream till I found myself again and knew it was all true.

"I'd found out that the car I was in was goin' to Mississippi and made out that it was for some saw-mill down there. It was switched 'round once or twice in the day, and I think once in the night, and was put on other trains, and the new brakeman had come 'round at different times. After I got the cigars I gave 'em one whenever they come 'round and this kep' 'em pretty good-natured. And so long as the car had switched off and I made up my mind they wouldn't find her the first day, I thought mebbe I'd better stay right in it and go to Mississippi. I didn't know nothin' 'bout Mississippi, except that it was south and a long ways off and settled with niggers, and that they made lumber down there. I used to see a good many cars from Mississippi when I was switchin' in the yards. The car was switched off quite a bit, and didn't go very fast, and it was four days before they landed it in Mississippi.

"They stopped right in the middle of the woods, and I made up my mind that this was about as good a place to stay as anywhere, if I could get a job, and I thought it wouldn't be a bad plan to try where they was sendin' the machine. It had been so easy for me to get down to Mississippi that I began to think that mebbe my luck had changed, and that the Lord had punished me all he was goin' to. So I went up to the mill and asked for a job. The foreman told me he'd give me one if I didn't mind workin' with niggers. I told him I didn't care anything 'bout that, I guessed they was as good as I was. So I started in. My whiskers was beginnin' to grow out some. You know I always kep' 'em shaved off, and now they was comin' out all over my face, and I made up my mind to let 'em grow. I went to work loadin' saw logs onto a little car that took 'em down into the mill. A great big stout nigger worked with me, and we took long poles and rolled the logs over onto the cars, and then it was rolled down into the mill and another one come up in its place. I found the only chance to board was in the big buildin' where all the hands lived. I thought this wa'n't a bad place. Most of the people boardin' there was niggers, but there was a few white fellers, and I naturally got acquainted with 'em.

"I'd been there a week or two when some one brought a Chicago paper into the house. It was covered with great big headlines and had my picture on the front page. It told all 'bout some boys findin' her and about the neighbors hearin' me call her a damned bitch, and about the kid wakin' up in the mornin' and goin' out in the street to hunt its ma. Then it offered a thousand dollars reward in great big letters.

"My whiskers had grown out a good deal and I didn't look so very much like the picture. Anyhow I don't think newspaper pictures look much like anybody. Still, of course, I was awful scart at that. My best chum read the piece all over out loud to me after we got through work, and he said it beat all what a place Chicago was; that such things as that was always happenin' in Chicago; and that Jackson must have been an awful bad man—wouldn't I hate to meet him out in the woods some place! A man like that would rather kill anybody than eat. I didn't say much about it, but of course I didn't contradict him. But I simply couldn't talk very much myself. He said he wished he could get the one thousand dollars, but no such luck would ever come to him.

"When I'd come there I said my name was Jones, because 'twas the easiest one I could think of; there was a butcher right near us that was named Jones, and it popped into my head at the time. Some of 'em asked me where I was from, and I told 'em Cincinnati. I didn't know much about Cincinnati, except that we used to get cars from there, and so I knew something 'bout the roads that went to it. I managed to get hold of the paper and burn it up without any one seein' me. But after it came I didn't feel so easy as I did before. I stayed there about a month workin' at the mill and pickin' up what I could about the country, and then I began to think my chum was gettin' suspicious of me. He kep' askin' me a good many questions about what I'd worked at and where'bouts I had worked, and how I got there from Cincinnati and a lot of questions about the town, and I thought he was altogether too inquisitive, and of course I would have told him so if I had dared. Finally I thought the other fellers was gettin' suspicious, too, and I thought they kind of watched me and asked a good many questions. So one time right after I got my pay I made up my mind to leave. I didn't wait to say nothin' to any one, but jumped onto a freight train, and went on about fifty miles or so south to a railroad crossin' and then I jumped off, and took another train east. Along next day I saw a little town where there was another saw mill, so I stopped off and asked for a job. I didn't have no trouble goin' to work, so long as I was willin' to work with the niggers, and I stayed there two or three weeks, same as the other place, and then I thought the boss began to notice me. He asked me a lot of questions about where I come from, and 'most everything else he could think of. I told him I come from St. Louis, but

I didn't know much more 'bout that place than I did 'bout Cincinnati, and I guess he didn't neither. But as soon as pay-day come I made up my mind I'd better start, so I took the few duds I'd got together and jumped on another train goin' further yet, and went away. Finally I stopped at a little town that looked rather nice and started out to get a job.

"Ever since I got off the first train I always looked pretty sharp at every one to make out whether they was watchin' me or not. Then I always got hold of all the newspapers I could find to see if there was anything more about me. I found another Chicago paper in the depot, and it still had my picture and the offer of a thousand dollars reward, and said I must have took one of the freight trains that left the yards, and would most likely be in the south or in the west. I didn't like to stay there any longer after seein' that paper, but I managed to fold it up the best I could, and just as quick as I got a chance I tore it to pieces and threw it away. Then I thought mebbe I'd better get back away from the railroad. So I seen an old darkey that looked kind of friendly and I asked him about the country. He told me a good deal about it and I started out to walk to where he said there was some charcoal pits. I found the place and managed to get a chance to work burnin' wood and tendin' fires. It was awful black sooty work, but I didn't care nothin' about that. The main thing with me was bein' safe. I had a pardner who worked with me keepin' up the fires and lookin' after the pits at night, and it looked kind of nice with the red fires of the pits lightin' up the woods and ever'-thing all 'round lookin' just like a picture. When we got through in the mornin' you couldn't tell us from darkies, we was so covered with smoke and burnt wood. We boarded in a little shanty with an old nigger lady that fed us on hominy and fried chicken, and we didn't have much of any place to sleep that was very good.

"After I'd been there two or three days I got pretty well acquainted with my pardner. One day he asked me where I was from. I never said nothin' to anybody 'bout where I come from, or where I was goin', or asked them any questions about themselves. I just worked steady at my job, and all I thought of was keepin' still in hopes it would wear off in time, and I could start over new. I used to dream a good deal about her and the boy, and sometimes I'd think we was back there in Chicago all livin' together and ever'thing goin' all right. Then I would dream that I was out with the boys to a caucus, or goin' 'round the saloons campaignin' with the alderman. Then I'd dream about fightin' her and hittin' her on the head with the poker, and it seemed as if I throwed her in Lake Michigan. Then I'd dream about the boy and my learnin' him his letters, and his bein' with me in the wagon when we was peddlin' potatoes, and about the horse, the old one that died, and the last one I got at the renderin'-place. Then I'd kind of get down to the peddlin', and go over the whole route in my sleep, hollerin' out 'po-ta-toes!' all along the streets on the west side where I used to go, and the old Italian women and the Bohemian ladies and all the rest would be out tryin' to get 'em cheaper and tellin' me how I'd charged too much. Then I seen the old lady that I give the half peck to, and could hear her ask all the saints to bless me. Then I stopped into the butcher-shop and got the steak, and ever'thing I ever done kep' comin' back to me, only not quite the same as it is in real life. You know how 'tis in a dream; you want to go somewhere and somethin' kind of holds your leg and you can't go. Or you want to do somethin' and no matter how hard you try somethin' is always gettin' in front of you and hinderin' you and keepin' you back. Well, that's the way 'twas with all my dreams; nothin' turned out right and I always come back to where I killed her and throwed her in the lake, till I was almost 'fraid to go to sleep, and then I was 'fraid I'd holler or talk in my sleep. And my chum slep' in the same room with me and I was 'fraid mebbe he'd find it out, so I never dared to go to sleep until after he did, and then I was always 'fraid I'd holler and say somethin' and wake him up and that he'd find out 'bout me and what I'd done.

"Well, as I was sayin', after I'd been there three or four days we was down to the pits one night tendin' to the fires, and we got to talkin' and tellin' stories to pass the time away, and at last he asked me where I was from, and I said St. Louis. He said he was from the north too; I didn't ask him where he'd come from, but he told me Chicago. I was almost scart to death when he mentioned the place. I didn't ask no questions nor say a word, but he kep' on talkin' so I kind of moved 'round a little and leaned up against a pine tree so's the light couldn't shine right in my face, for I didn't know what he might say. He told me that he come down here every winter for his health; that Chicago was so cold and changeable in the winter; that he worked in the stock-yards when he was there and he always went back just as soon as he dared, that there wa'n't no place in the world like Chicago, and he was always awful lonesome when he was away, and he wouldn't ever leave it if he could only stand the climate. He said there was always somethin' goin' on in Chicago; a feller could get a run for his money no matter what kind of a game he played; that if he wanted to have a little sport, there was the pool-rooms and plenty of other places; that if he didn't have much money he could get a little game in the back end of a cigar store, or he could shoot craps; if he wanted a bigger game there was Powers' & O'Brien's and O'Leary's, and if that wa'n't enough, then there was the Board of Trade. There was always lots of excitement in Chicago, too. There was races and elections and always strikes, and ever'-thing goin' on. Then there was more murders and hangin's in Chicago than in any other city. Take that car-barn case; it couldn't never have happened anywhere except in Chicago. And the Luetgert case, where the feller boiled his wife up in the sausage-vat so that there wa'n't nothin' left but one or two toe-nails, but one doctor identified her by them, and swore they was toe-nails and belonged to a woman about her size;

one of 'em had seen her over at a picnic and remembered her, and he was pretty sure that the toe-nails was hers. Then that Jackson case was the latest; that happened just a little while before he left, and the papers was full of that one. Jackson was a peddler and he went 'round all day and drunk at all the saloons just so he could get up nerve enough to kill her. He thought she had some property and he'd get it if she was out of the way, so he killed her and took her off and put her in a hole where he thought no one could find her; but they did, and now one of the papers had offered a thousand dollars reward for him, and they were lookin' for him all over the United States. He said as how he took a Chicago paper and kep' posted on everything and read it every day and wouldn't be without it for a minute. And then he asked me if I hadn't never been to Chicago, and why I didn't go. I told him mebbe I would some time, but I'd always been kind of 'fraid to go. I didn't say much but got the subject changed as soon as possible, and managed to put in the rest of the night the best I could, and then went home, and after he'd gone to sleep I packed my valise and paid the nigger lady and told her I had enough of that job and started off afoot without waitin' for my pay.

"I went straight down the road for two or three miles till I come to where another road crossed, then I turned off to the left. I didn't have any reason for turnin', except it seemed as if that would take me more out of the way. I didn't see any one along the road except now and then some old nigger. I walked several miles, and there didn't 'pear to be no one livin' on the road except niggers with little shanties same as the one I left in Chicago. I stopped once and asked an old darkey lady for somethin' to eat and she give me some fried chicken and a piece of corn bread and I sat and et it, and a whole lot of woolly-headed little pickaninnies sat and looked at me every mouthful. One of 'em was about the size of my kid, and made me think of him a good deal; but he didn't look nothin' like him. I guess 'twas just because he was a boy and about the age of mine. After I et the chicken and the bread I started on and traveled all day without seein' any one, except niggers, or stoppin' anywhere except to get a drink in a little stream. When it begun to be dark I commenced to think what I'd do for the night, and watched out for a place to stay. So after while I saw an old shack 'side of the road and went in. There was some straw and I was so tired that I laid down and went right to sleep.

"All night I dreamed about bein' follered. First I thought I was out in a woods and some hounds was chasin' me, and I heard 'em bayin' way back on my trail and knew they's comin' for me. I run to a little stream and follered it up same as I used to read in Indian stories, and then started on again, and after a while I didn't hear 'em any more. Then first thing I knew they commenced bayin' again and I could tell that they'd struck my trail, so I run just as fast as ever I could and the bayin' kep' gettin' louder'n louder, and I run through bushes and brush and ever'thing, and they kep' gainin' on me till they was so close that I got to a little tree where I could almost reach the branches and I got hold of 'em and pulled myself up and got ahead of the hounds, but they come up and set down around the tree and howled and howled so they'd be heard all through the woods, and I knew it was all up with me; and then I woke up and found that I was in the barn and no one 'round except a cow or a horse that was eatin' over in a corner. So I tried to go to sleep again. Then I dreamed that the policemen and detectives was after me, and first it seemed as if I was runnin' down a street and the police was right behind, and then I turned down an alley and they hollered to me to stop or they'd shoot, but I didn't stop, and they shot at me and hit me in the leg, and I fell down and they come up and got me, and then it seemed as if I was on the cars and detectives was follerin' me ever'where, and whenever I stopped them detectives somehow knew where I was, and they'd come to the place, and I got away and went somewhere else, and then they'd turn up there, all ready to arrest me, and I couldn't go anywhere except they'd follow me. And I kind of saw her face, and she seemed to be follerin' me too, only she didn't seem to have any legs or much of anything, except just her face and a kind of long white train and she just come wherever I was, without walkin' or ridin', but just come, and she always seemed to know just the right place no matter how careful I hid, and when they got all ready to nab me I woke up. By that time it was daylight and there was a darkey there in the barn feedin' a mule, and he said, 'Hello, boss!' just as friendly, and asked me where I was goin'. I told him I was lookin' for a job, and he told me he thought that over about four miles to the town I could get a job. So I told him all right, and asked him if he could give me somethin' to eat. He took me into the house and gave me some chicken and some corn-cakes and told me if I would wait a while he'd hitch up the mule and take me into town, that he was goin' anyway. I thanked him and told him I was in a hurry to get to work, and guessed I wouldn't wait. I'd got so I was 'fraid to talk with anybody. I thought they'd ask me where I was from, and tell me somethin' 'bout Chicago, and mebbe show me a newspaper with my picture in it.

"Then I went on down the road till I come to a nice town in the middle of big pine trees. It was full of fine white houses and a few brick stores, and two or three great big hotels. I asked a nigger what the place was and he told me it was Thompson, and was a winter resort for Yankees who come there for their lungs; that they spent lots of money and that was what made the place so big.

"I always liked to talk with the niggers; they never asked me any questions, and I never was 'fraid that they'd been in Chicago, and I didn't really think they took any of the papers, for they didn't know how to read. Well, I just took one look at Thompson and then went as far from the hotels as I could, and kep' away from the stores, for I was sure the place was full of people from Chicago, and that all the newspapers would be there, too. I didn't stop a minute over where all the nice houses was. I seen lots of people out on the porches and settin' in hammocks and loafin' 'round, and I knew they was from Chicago. Then I went along across a little stream and come to a lot of poor tumbled-down houses and tents, and I knew they was the niggers' quarters, so I went into a little store kep' by an old fat nigger lady and bought a bag of crackers and asked her about the roads.

"Before this I made up my mind to go to Cuba. I remembered readin' all about it at the time of the war, when a lot of them stock-yards boys went to fight, and I thought that I'd be so far away that I might be safe, so I knew that I had to go to the Gulf of Mexico, and I kep' on that way. I didn't dare to take the railroads any more, but just thought I'd walk, so I kep' straight on down the road all day until I got a long ways from Thompson. I didn't dare to stop for work, for I'd got it into my head that every one was after me, and if I waited any more I'd get caught. My shoes was gettin' pretty near wore out and I knew they wouldn't last much longer, and I hadn't got more'n four dollars left, and I knew if I didn't come to the Gulf pretty soon I'd just have to go to work.

"That night I stopped at another old shack,

and had about the same kind of dream I did the night before, only I was runnin', and every time I pretty near got away a cramp would come in my leg and pull me back and give 'em a chance to ketch me, and they seemed to come just the same without runnin' or flyin', or anything, and always she'd come just where I was. Still I got through the night and a nigger lady gave me somethin' to eat, and I went on.

"I began to look awful ragged and shabby. My coat was torn and awful old and black where I'd been workin' in the charcoal pit. I'd changed my shirt, and washed the one I had on in a little stream, but the buttons was gettin' off and I was tyin' 'em up with strings. My pants was all wore out 'long the bottom, and my shoes pretty near all knocked to pieces. As for my stockin's—you couldn't call 'em stockin's at all, and I'd made up my mind to get a new pair the next store I come to, but I didn't like to stop in town.

"Along about noon I got to a little place and, of course, I was lookin' pretty bad. Some o' the dogs commenced barkin' at me as soon as ever I got into town. I stopped at a house to get somethin' to eat, and a white lady come to the door and told me to go 'way, that I was a tramp, and that she'd set the dog on me, and I ran as fast as I could. I went down the street and a good many boys follered me, and I began to get scart; so I went through the town as fast as I could, but I see some people was follerin' after me, and one that rode on a horse. So I took to the fields and made for a clump of trees that I saw off to the right. I run just as fast as ever I could and when I looked back I saw some people was follerin' me through the field. I went straight to the woods and ran through 'em, and got pretty badly scratched up, and my clothes tore worse'n they was before. Then I run into a swamp just beyond and two or three men ran 'round on the other side of the swamp and I knew it was all up, and I might just as well surrender and go back.

"I was so scart I didn't care much what they done, so when the one in front asked me to surrender or he'd shoot, I come out to where he was, and he put his hand on me kind of rough and said I was under arrest for bein' a tramp, and to come with him.

"Then he took me back to town with all the men follerin', and when we got up into the edge of the place 'most all the boys, black and white, turned in and follered too. They took me to a little buildin' over on the side of the town, and went down stairs into the cellar and opened an iron door and put me in. There wa'n't no light except one window which was covered with iron bars, and they locked the door and went away and left me there alone."

VIII

"I WAS locked up in the cellar for a long time before any one came to talk with me. I looked 'round to see if there was any chance to get out, but I seen it couldn't be done. I thought it wa'n't hardly worth while to try. Honestly it seemed a kind of relief to be ketched and know I didn't have to run any more. I didn't know why they arrested me, but I s'posed they just thought I'd done something and they'd try to find out what is was, so I thought about what I'd do, and made up my mind I hadn't better say much.

"After a while some fellers come down to see me and took me up in the office. One of 'em was the marshal and another was a lawyer or police-judge or somethin' of that kind. They said they wanted to fill out some sort of a paper about who I was and where I come from and what my business was and who my father and mother was, and what my religion was, and whether I ever drank, or smoked cigarettes, and the color of my hair and eyes, and how much I weighed, and a lot of things like that. So I told 'em I was from St. Louis, and guessed at the rest of the answers the best I could. Only I told 'em I never knew who my father and mother was. They wa'n't satisfied with my answers and fired a lot more questions at me. And then they told me they thought I lied, and they'd put me in the lock-up until mornin', so they put me back there and give me a plate o' scraps for supper, and a straw bed to sleep on, and then went away.

"Somehow I slept better that night than I had since I'd run away. I rather thought it was all up and only a question of time when I'd get back here, but I knew where I stood and wa'n't so scart. I've slep' fine ever since I was here, only the time when the jury was out and when I was waitin' for the Supreme Court, and some special times like that. As near as I can find out most of 'em does when they know it's all off, just like people with a cancer or consumption, or when they're awful old. They get used to it and sleep just the same unless they have a pain, or somethin'. They don't lay awake thinkin' they're goin' to die. And after all, I guess if people done that there wouldn't any of 'em sleep much. For 'tain't very long with anybody, and bein' sentenced to death ain't much differ'nt from dyin' without a sentence. In one way ever'body's sentenced to death. Of course, I s'pose it's a little shorter and still that ain't always the case. There's two fellers that I knew died since I come here; one of 'em had pneumonia, and the other was a switchman that thought the engine was on the other side-track. John Murphy was his name. Still—I guess my time's pretty near come now.

"Well, in the mornin' the marshal came in and brought me some breakfast. Then he took me up to the office again. He waited a few minutes till the judge come, and then they commenced firin' questions at me. They asked me how I got from St. Louis to where I was. That kind of puzzled me, for I didn't exactly know where I was. I answered it the best I could; but I know I didn't get it right. They told me I hadn't got over lyin' and I'd have to be shut up some more. Then they asked me what public buildin's there was in St. Louis. I made a guess and told 'em the court-house and state-house. They laughed at this, and said St. Louis wa'n't the capital of Missouri. And of course I didn't argue with 'em about that. Then they wanted to know how I come there and I said I walked. And they wanted to know what places I come through and I couldn't tell 'em. Then they asked me where I had walked, and I couldn't tell 'em that; and they asked me how far I'd walked, and I told 'em not very far, and they laughed at my clothes and shoes and said they was 'most wore out, and they didn't believe it, and told me again that they thought I was lyin' and I'd have to stay there till I learnt how to tell the truth. Then I got mad and said I hadn't done nothin' and they hadn't any right to keep me, and I wouldn't answer any more questions; that they didn't believe anything I said anyhow and it wa'n't any use, and to go ahead and do what they pleased with me.

"Then the marshal went to his desk and got a lot of photographs and hand-bills tellin' about murderers and robbers and burglars and pick-pockets and ever'thing else, that was sent to him from all over the country, and he took 'em and looked 'em all over and then looked at me. Then he sorted out a dozen or so and stared at me more particular than before. I seen what he had in his hand; I seen one of 'em was my picture; only I was smooth-faced and now my whiskers had got long. He made me take off my clothes and looked me over careful, and found where I had broke my leg the time that I caught my foot between the rails when I thought I was goin' to be run over. You remember the time? I wish now I had. Then he let me put on my clothes, and he went over all the descriptions just as careful as he could, and he found that the hand-bill told about a broken leg; then he looked at my face again, and then he asked me when I'd shaved last, and I told him I never shaved. Then he wanted to know how tall I was, and I told him I didn't know, so he measured me by standin' me up 'gainst the wall and markin' the place. I tried to scrooch down as much as I could without him noticin' it; but he said it was just 'bout what the hand-bill had it. Then he asked me how much I weighed, and I told him I hadn't been weighed for years. So he called some one to help him, and they put some han'-cuffs on one arm and fastened the other to the marshal and took me over to a store, and made me stand on the scales till I got weighed. He said I weighed just a little bit less than the han'-bill made it, and that if I'd walked from Chicago that would account for the difference. Then he looked over my clothes, but he couldn't find any marks on 'em.

"Then he sent down for the barber and told him to shave me. I objected to that and told him he hadn't any right to do it; that I wasn't charged with any crime, and he said it didn't make no difference, he was goin' to do it any way. So I knew it wa'n't no use, and I set down and let the barber shave me. Of course I knew it would all be up as soon as I got shaved. But I didn't care so very much if it was; it wa'n't any worse than runnin' all the time and bein' 'fraid of ever'-one you met and knowin' you'd be ketched at last.

"Well, after the barber got through shavin' me, the marshal took the picture and held it up side of my face, and any one could see 'twas me. He was so glad he almost shouted. And he told the police judge that he'd got one of the most dangerous criminals in the whole United States, and he was entitled to one thousand dollars reward. I never see a boy feel so good over anythin' as he did over ketchin' me. He said that now he could pay off the mortgage on his house and get his girl piano lessons, and run for sheriff next fall. When he told me I was Jackson, I denied it and said I never knew anything about Chicago, and was never there in my life. He didn't pay any attention to this, but wired to Chicago, givin' a full description of me. Of course, it wa'n't long before he got back word that I was Jackson, and to hold me till they sent some one down.

"After the marshal found out who I was he

treated me a good deal better'n before. He got me nice fried chicken 'most every meal, and always coffee or tea and corn-cakes, and I couldn't complain of the board. Then he got my clothes washed and give me some new pants and shoes and fixed me up quite nice. He come in and visited with me a good deal and seemed real sociable and happy. He give me cigars to smoke and sometimes a drink o' whiskey, and treated me as if he really liked me. I expect he couldn't help feelin' friendly to me, because he thought of that one thousand dollars, and that he wouldn't of got it if I hadn't killed her, and in one way a good deal as if I done it on his account. Of course he wa'n't really glad I done it, but so long as I done it, he was glad I come his way. I s'pose he hadn't anything against me any more'n a cat has against a mouse that it ketches and plays with till it gets ready to eat it up. His business was ketchin' people just like the cat's is ketchin' rats. Seems to me, though, I'd hate to be in his business, even if it is a bad lot you've got to ketch. Still he watched me closer'n ever, even if he was good to me. He didn't mean to let that thousand dollars get away. He kep' some one 'round the jail all the time, and he got some extra bars on the windows, and when he come to see me or talk with me he always brought some one with him so I couldn't do anything to him. He needn't worried so much, for I was clean tired out and discouraged, and I felt better in there than I had any time since I killed her. Bein' out of jail ain't necessar'ly liberty. If you're 'fraid all the time and have got to dodge and keep hid and can't go where you want to and are runnin' away all the time, you might just as well be shut up, for you ain't free.

"Soon as the marshal found out who I was, it didn't take the news long to travel 'round the town, and it seemed as if ever'one there come to the lock-up to see me. The boys used to come up 'round the windows and kind of stay back, as if they thought I might reach out and ketch 'em, but I always kep' as far away as I could. Then the people would come down with the marshal to the cell when he brought my supper and look in at me to see me eat, and try to get me to come up and talk to 'em and watch me same as you've seen 'em look at bears when they was feedin' up at Lincoln Park, and they'd point to me and say, 'That's him; just see his for'head. Wouldn't I hate to get caught out alone with him? Any one could see what he is by lookin' at him. I bet they make short work of him when they get him to Chicago!' I always kep' back as far as I could for I didn't want to be seen. No one had ever looked at me or paid any attention to me before, or said anything about me, and I hadn't ever expected to have my name or picture in the paper, or to have people come and see me, and anyhow not this way.

"Of course, I knew well enough that it wouldn't last long, and that they'd be here for me in two or three days. I can't tell you just how I felt. I knew I was caught, and that there wa'n't much chance for me. I knew all the evidence would be circumstantial, still I knew I done it, and luck never had come my way anyhow, so I didn't have much hopes that 'twould now. Then I began to feel as if it might as well be over. If I was goin' to be hung, I might just as well be hung and done with it. There wa'n't any kind of a show for me any more, and it wa'n't any use to fight. Then I began to figger on how long 'twould take. I knew there was cases where it took years, but I always thought them cases must have been where they had lots of money and could hire high-priced lawyers. And I hadn't got any money, and the newspapers had said so much about my case that I was sure that they wouldn't give me much chance or any more than the law allowed.

"Well, inside of two days some fellers come down from the sheriff's office in Chicago. I didn't know either one of 'em, but they had all kinds of pictures and descriptions and said there wa'nt any doubt about who I was, and said I might as well own up and be done with it. But I didn't see any use of ownin' up to anything, so I wouldn't answer any questions or say much one way or another. Then they explained to me that they hadn't any right to take me out of the state without a requisition from the gov'nor, and it would take a week or so to get that, and I might just as well go back with them without puttin' 'em to this bother; that it always looked better when any one went back themselves, and anyhow I'd be kep' here in jail till they got a requisition. So I told 'em all right, I'd just as soon go back to Chicago as anywhere, and I hadn't done nothin' that I had to be 'fraid of, and was ready to go as soon as they was. So they stayed till the next mornin' and then han'-cuffed me and put me between 'em and led me down to the depot. Before I left the lock-up the marshal give me a good breakfast and some cigars and shook hands with me, and said he hoped I'd have a pleasant journey.

"When I went down to the depot it seemed as if the whole town, black and white, had turned out to see me, and ever'one was pointin' to me and sayin', 'That's him; that's him.' 'He looks it, don't he?' And pretty soon the train come up and the officers and conductor kep' the crowd back while they took me into the smokin'-car. It seemed as if ever'one in the car and on the whole train knew who I was and just what I'd done, and they all come up to the smokin'-car to get a look at me, and pass remarks about me, and ever'one seemed glad to think I was caught and was goin' to be hung.

"It ain't no use to tell you all about the trip home. It didn't take me so long to come back as it did to go 'way. At pretty near ever' station there was a crowd out to see the train, and all of 'em tried to get a look at me. The conductor and brakemen all pointed me out and the people come to the doors and stood up before the windows and did ever'thing they could think of to see me. The detectives treated me all right. They give me all I could eat and talked with me a good deal. They didn't ask many questions, and told me I needn't say any more'n I had a mind to, but they told me a good deal about politics and how that the alderman was runnin' again, and all that was goin' on in Chicago, and where all they'd been huntin' for me since I run away. I had to sit up at night. One of 'em kep' han'-cuffed to me all night and another han'cuff was fastened to the seat. I don't s'pose they could've made it any more comfortable and see that I didn't run away. But still I don't ever want to take that kind of a ride again and I s'pose I never will.

"I felt queer when we began to get back into Chicago. In some ways I always liked the city; I guess ever'one does, no matter how rough it is. And I couldn't help feelin' kind of good to see the streets and fact'ries and shops again; and still I felt bad, too. I knew that ever'one in the town was turned against me, and I didn't have a friend anywhere. We'd got the Chicago papers as we'd come along and they was full of all kinds of stories and pictures about me, and some things that I'd said, 'though I'd never talked a word to any one.

"The papers said that they hoped there'd be none of the usual long delays in tryin' my case, that I was a brutal murderer, and there wa'n't no use of spendin' much time over me. Of course, I ought to have a fair and impartial trial, but I ought to be hung without delay, and no sentimental notoriety-huntin' people ought to be allowed to see me. They wished that a judge could be found who had the courage to do his duty, and do it right off quick. I had already been indicted, and there wa'n't nothin' to do but place me on trial next day, and the verdict would be reached in a few days more. It was unfortunate that the law allowed one hundred days before a murderer could be hung after trial; that the next legislature must change it to ten days; that would be plenty of time for any one to show that a mistake had been made in their trial, even if he was locked up all the time. The papers said how that the Anti-Crimes Committee was to be congratulated on havin' found a good lawyer to assist the state in the prosecution, and that the lawyer was a good public spirited man and ought to be well paid for his disagreeable work.

"The papers told all about the arrest down in Georgia, and how the marshal and a force of citizens followed me into the swamp and what a desperate fight I made, and how many people I'd knocked down and 'most killed, until I was finally overpowered and taken in irons to the county jail.

"I can't make you understand how I felt when they was bringin' me into town. We come along down the old canal where we used to stone the frogs and the geese and all along the places where us boys used to play. Then we come down through the yards where I used to work, and right past the house where I left that night with the kid sleepin' in the bedroom. That was the hardest part of all the trip, and I tried to turn away when we come down along back of the barn by the alley; but it seemed as if something kind of drew my eyes around that way, and I couldn't keep 'em off'n the spot. And I thought about ever'thing I done there just in a flash, and even wondered how long the old horse was tied in the barn before they found him, and whether he got all the potatoes et up before he was took away. But I looked away as quick as I could and watched all the streets as we passed, to see if I could see any one I knew. I felt pretty sure that I wouldn't leave Chicago again, and I guess I never will.

"Pretty soon they pulled into the big depot, and the train stopped and we got off. I wa'n't expectin' nothin' in the station, but when we landed the whole place was filled back of the gate, and I could see that they was lookin' for me. The crowd was about like one that I was in down there once when McKinley come to Chicago. A squad of policemen come down to meet us, and they got us in the middle of the bunch and hurried us into a patrol wagon. I could hear the crowd sayin', 'That's him; that's the murderer; let's lynch him!'—'He don't deserve a trial! Let's hang him first and then try him'—'The miserable brute!' 'The contemptible coward!'—I guess if it hadn't been for all the policemen I'd have been lynched, and mebbe 'twould have been just as well. 'Twouldn't have taken so long, nor cost so much money. Anyhow, I wish now they'd done it and then it would be all over; and now—well, 'twon't be long.

"There was a lot of people in the street and every one of 'em seemed to know who was in the patrol-wagon, and they walked all the way over, and lots of little boys follered the wagon clear to the jail; then the newsboys on the street kep' yellin', 'All 'bout the capture of Jim Jackson! Extra paper!' and it seemed as if the whole town was tryin' to kill me. Somehow I hadn't realized how 'twas as I come 'long, and, in fact, ever since I went away. Of course I knew how bad the killin' was, and how ever'one must feel, and how I wished I hadn't done it, and how I'd have done anything on earth to make it different, but all the time I'd been away from the people that knew all about it, and I didn't somehow realize what they'd do. But when I come back and seen it all I felt just as if there was a big storm out on the lake and I was standin' on the shore and all the waves was comin' right over me and carryin' me away.

"Well, they didn't lose any time but drove as fast as they could down Dearborn Street over the bridge to the county jail. Then they hustled me right out and took me straight through the crowd up to the door; the Dearborn Street door (that's the one you came in, I s'pose), and they didn't wait hardly a minit to book me, but hurried me up stairs and locked me in a cell, and I haven't seen the outside of the jail since, and I don't s'pose I ever will."

Jim stopped as if the remembrance of it all had overpowered him. Hank didn't know what to say, so he got up and walked a few turns back and forth along the cell, trying to get it all through his clouded mind. Such a night as this he had never dreamed of, and could not yet realize what it meant. The long story and the intense suffering seemed to have taken all the strength that Jim had left.

Hank turned to him with an effort to give him some consolation. "Say, Jim, don't take it too hard. You know there ain't much in it for any of us, and most people has more trouble than anything else. Lay down a little while; you can tell me the rest pretty soon."

"No," Jim answered, "I ain't got through; I can't waste any time. It must be gettin' along toward mornin', and you see I don't know just when it'll be. They seem to think it's treatin' us better if they don't tell us when, only just the day. Then you know, they can come in any time after midnight. They could break in now if they wanted to, but I s'pose they'll give me my breakfast first, though they won't wait long after that. Well, I ain't got any right to complain, and I don't mean to, but I s'pose I feel like any one else would."

Just then a strange dull sound echoed through the silent corridors. Hank started with a nervous jerk. It sounded like a rope or strap suddenly pulled up short and tight.

"What's that?" Hank asked. Jim's face was pale for a moment, and his breath was short and heavy.

"Don't you know? That's the bag of sand."

"What bag of sand?" Hank asked.

"Why, they always try the rope that way, to see if it's all right. If they don't, it's liable to break, and they'd have to hang 'em over again.

They take a bag of sand that weighs just about the same as a man and tie the rope to the sand, and then knock the door out and the sand falls. I guess the rope's all right; I hope so. I don't want 'em to make any mistake. It'll be bad enough to be hung once. I wonder how I'll stand it. I hope I don't make a scene. But I don't really think any one ought to be blamed no matter what they do when they're gettin' hung, do you?

"It seems to me, though, that they might be a better way to kill any one. I think shootin' would be better'n this way. That's the way they kill steers down to the stock-yards and I don't believe the Humane Society would let 'em hang 'em up by the neck. I should think 'twould be better to take some cell that's air-tight and put 'em to bed in there and then turn on the gas. But I s'pose any way would seem bad enough. Did you ever stop to think how you'd like to die? I guess nobody could pick any way that they wanted to go, and mebbe we'd all rather take chances; but I don't believe anybody'd pick hangin'. It seems to me the very worst way anybody could die. I wonder how they commenced it in the first place. Well, I can't help it by thinkin' it over. I've done that often enough already, goodness knows. I believe I'll ask the guard for another drink before I tell any more."

The guard came at the first call.

"Sure, you can have all the whiskey you want. I was just down to the office a little while ago. Take this bottle. I think it's pretty smooth, but it's a little weak. Guess the clerk poured some water in, thinkin' it was goin' to the ladies' ward. You'd better take a pretty big drink to do you any good."

Jim thanked him as he took the bottle, and then inquired:

"Did you go down to the telephone again to see whether there had anything come over to the telegraph-office?"

"No—I didn't," the guard answered, "but I'll go back pretty soon. They keep open all night. It's early yet, anyhow."

Jim offered the bottle to his friend. Hank took a good drink, which he needed after the excitement of the night. Then he passed the bottle back to Jim.

"If I was you I'd drink all that's left; it's good, but it's pretty weak, all right. I'm sure you'd feel better to take it all."

Jim raised it to his lips, tipped his head back and held the bottle almost straight until the last drop had run slowly down his throat.

IX

Jim laid the bottle on the bed and then sat down on his chair.

"My head begins to swim some but I guess I can finish the story all right. I know I'm pretty longwinded. Still I guess I can't talk very much more if I wanted to. I'm glad the whiskey's beginnin' to get in its work; I don't believe I'll have much trouble gettin' so drunk that I won't know whether I'm goin' to a hangin' or a primary.

"Let me see; Oh, yes, they hustled me into a cell and locked me up. I guess they thought best not to waste much time, for a good many people had got together on the outside.

"I think 'twas on Friday they put me in. There wa'n't nothin' done on Saturday; but on Sunday they let us all go to church up in the chapel. They kep' me pretty well guarded as if I might do somethin' in the church, but there wa'n't no way to get out if I wanted to. The preacher told us about the prodigal son, and how he repented of all his wanderin's and sins and come back home, and how glad his father was to see him, and how he treated him better'n any of the rest that hadn't never done wrong. He said that's the way our

Heavenly Father would feel about us, if we repented, and that it didn't matter what we'd done—after we repented we was white as snow. One of the prisoners told me he was gettin' kind of tired of the prodigal son; that most every preacher that come told about the prodigal son just as if that story had been meant specially for them.

"Some of the prisoners seemed to like to go to church; some acted as if they understood all about it, and wanted to do better, and some of 'em seemed to go so as to get out of their cells. Anyhow I s'pose the people that run the jail thought 'twas a good thing and believed it was all so. But I know one feller that killed a man—he was kind of half-witted—and was tried the same as the rest of us when they had that crusade against crime. Of course they sentenced him to death. He got religion and used to pray all the time, and used to talk religion to all the rest of the fellers, and ever'one said that he was really sorry and was fully converted and was as pure as a little child. But they took him out and hung him anyway. It don't quite seem as if they believed what the preacher said themselves, or they wouldn't hang a feller when he's turned right, and when God was goin' to treat him like all the rest after he gets to heaven.

"When I went back to my cell, I begun thinkin' about what I'd do. Of course I knew you can't get any show without a lawyer, and I knew that I might just about as well not have any as to have one that wa'n't smart. I didn't know any lawyer except the one that charged me ten dollars for nothin', and of course I wouldn't have him. But one of the guards was kind of nice and friendly to me and I thought I'd ask him. He told me that gettin' a lawyer was a pretty hard matter. Of course, my case was a celebrated one, and would advertise a lawyer, but the best ones didn't need no advertisin' and the others wa'n't no good. He told me that Groves was the best fighter, but it wa'n't no use to try to get him for he'd got more'n he could do, and most of his time was took up prosecutin' people for stealin' coal from the railroads, except once in a while when some rich banker or politician got into trouble. Then he took a good slice of what he'd got saved up. I asked him 'bout some others and he told me the same story of all the rest that amounted to anything. I told him I hadn't got no money, and I thought the horse and wagon and furniture was took on the chattel-mortgage before this, and he said he s'posed the court would have to appoint some one and I might just about as well defend myself.

"Monday mornin' they come to the jail and told me I had to go before the judge. I didn't s'pose 'twould come so soon, for I knew somethin' about how slow the courts was. You remember when Jimmy Carroll was killed by the railroad? Well, that's more'n three years ago, and the case ha'n't been tried yet. I was su'prised and didn't know what to do, but there wa'n't much to do. They come after me and I had to go; so I put on my coat and vest and they han'-cuffed me to a couple of guards, and took me through some alleys and passages and over some bridges inside the buildin', and first thing I knew they opened a door and I came into a room packed full of people, and the judge settin' up on a big high seat with a desk in front of him, and lookin' awful solemn and kind of scareful. As soon as I stepped in there was a buzz all over the room, and ever'-body reached out their necks, and kind of got up on their chairs and looked at me. The guards took off my han'-cuffs and set me down in a chair 'side of a big table. And then one of 'em set back of me and another one right to my side.

"They waited a few minutes till ever'one got still, and then some feller got up and spoke to the judge and said 'People against Jackson.' The judge looked at me and said, just as solemn and hard as he could, 'Jackson, stand up.' Of course I done what he said, and then he looked the same way and said, 'Are you guilty or not guilty?' Of course I was kind of scared before all of them people; I'd never been called up in a crowd before, except a few times when I said a few words in the union where I knew all the boys. But these people were all against me, and anyhow it was an awful hard place to put a feller, so I stood still a minit tryin' to think what I ought to say, and whether some one was there that I could talk to. Finally the judge spoke up and says, 'The prisoner pleads not guilty.' 'Jackson, have you a lawyer?' and then I said: 'I hain't got no lawyer.' Then he asked if I wanted him to appoint one, and I told him I wished he would. He asked me who I'd have. Of course I thought I could choose any one I wanted, so I said Groves. Then he laughed and ever'one else laughed, and he said he guessed Groves had too much to do to bother with me. So I chose one or two more names I'd heard of, and he said none of 'em would do it neither. Then he said he'd give me till to-morrow to make up my mind who I wanted, and he told the bailiff to take me back to jail. So they put the han'-cuffs on and we went back through the alleys and over the bridges to the jail. When I got to my cell I asked the guard what he thought I ought to do about a lawyer, and he said that lots of lawyers had give him their cards and asked him to hand them to the prisoners and told him they would divide the fee, if they got any. They mostly wa'n't much good for the business. He said there was one young feller who seemed pretty smart, but he hadn't never had a case, but he'd probably work hard to get his name up. I told him that it didn't seem as if a lawyer ought to commence on a case like mine, and he said that wouldn't make any difference, most of the murder cases was defended by lawyers that was just startin'. There wa'n't hardly any one who was tried but was too poor to have a good lawyer. Then I told him to send me the young lawyer, and he did.

"The lawyer wa'n't a bad feller, and he seemed interested in the case, and was the first person I'd seen since I done it who wanted to help me. Of course I could see he was new at the business, like one of them green-horns that comes in the yards the first time and brings a stick to couple cars with; but I liked his face and seen he was honest. It didn't seem quite fair, though, that I should have a lawyer that hadn't never had a case. I didn't believe they'd take a young feller who was just out of a medicine-college and set him to cut off a leg all by himself, the first thing, or even take a country-jake and let him kill steers at the stock-yards, but I didn't see no way to help it, and I thought mebbe if I didn't take him I'd do worse instead of better. He asked me all about the case and seemed disappointed when I told him how it was; he said he was afraid there wa'n't much show, unless he claimed insanity. I told him I didn't see how he could make out that I was crazy; that I thought self-defense or somethin' like that would be better. He said he'd think it over till to-morrow, and talk with some of the professors at the college, and be in court in the mornin'. The next day they come for me right after breakfast, and put on the han'-cuffs and took me to court again. The same kind of a crowd was there as the day before, and I was pretty badly scart; but my lawyer was at the table with me, and he spoke to me real friendly, and that made me feel a little better. Then the judge called the case, and asked if I had a lawyer, and my lawyer spoke up and said he was goin' to defend me; so the judge said all right, and asked if the other side was ready. They said they was, and that they wanted the case tried right off. Then the judge asked my lawyer if he was ready and he said 'no,' that he'd just come into the case and hadn't had no chance to get it ready. Then the lawyer on the other side said that I was notified yesterday that I must be ready to-day and I didn't have anything to do but get ready; that they wanted to try it now; that next week he wanted to go to a picnic, and the week after to a convention, and it must be done now; then, there had been so many murders that no one was safe in Chicago, and the whole public was anxious to see the case tried at once. Besides there wa'n't any defense. I had killed her and run away, and wa'n't entitled to any consideration.

"My lawyer said it wouldn't be right to put me on trial without a chance to defend myself, that I couldn't get away yesterday to look up witnesses, and I had a right to a reasonable time; that he wanted at least four weeks to prepare the case. This seemed to make the judge mad. He said there wa'n't no excuse for any delay, but as this was such a clear case he wanted to give me every chance he could, so he would continue till next Monday. Then I was took back to the jail, and my lawyer met me over there and I told him ever' place I went the day I done it, and ever'one I saw, and all about her, and what she'd done to make me mad, and he said he'd go out himself and look it up, and do what he could, but he was 'fraid there wa'n't no chance. The papers had said so much and the citizens had got up a Crime Committee, and ever'one who was tried either went to the penitentiary or got hung.

"Ever'day the lawyer would come and ask me something 'bout the case, and tell me what he'd found out. He said he couldn't get any witnesses to say anything; that the man where I got the beefsteak was 'fraid to come and testify; that some one had been there from the State's Attorney's office and most scart him to death, and he was 'fraid of gettin' into trouble and gettin' mixed up with it himself, and anyway he didn't see as he'd do the case any good if he came. He said he couldn't find anything that helped him a bit. He'd been to the house, but the poker and everything that would do any good had been taken by the state, and he didn't know which way to turn. He kep' comin' back to my insanity, and asked me if any of my parents or grand-parents, or uncles or aunts or cousins, or any one else was crazy. I told him I didn't know anything 'bout them but I didn't think it was any use to try that. I knew what I was doin', all right. Then he told me if I had a hunderd dollars he could get a good doctor to swear I was crazy; but I hadn't any hunderd dollars of course, and besides I never thought 'twould do much good. So I told him that he wa'n't to blame for it, and to just do the best he could, and I'd be satisfied whichever way it went. I didn't expect much myself anyhow. He said he'd have me plead guilty and the judge would most likely give me a life-sentence, only since this crusade against crime the judges dassent do that; there was so much said about it in the newspapers, and they was all 'fraid of what the papers said. He told me that he didn't believe it was anything more than second-degree murder anyhow, but there wa'n't any chance now, the way public opinion was.

"I begun to get pretty well acquainted with the prisoners in the jail and some of 'em was real nice and kind and wanted to do all they could to help ever'one that was in trouble. Of course some of 'em was pretty desp'rate, and didn't seem to care much for anything. Then there was some that had been in jail ten and fifteen times, and been in the penitentiary, and ever'where, and just as soon as they got out they got right back in again; they didn't seem to learn anything by goin' to prison, and it didn't seem to do them any hurt. They said they'd just as soon be there as anywhere else.

"But one thing I noticed a good deal that I never thought anything about until that feller come and spoke, that was how that the outsiders was really the ones that got punished the worst. It was sickenin' to see how some of them poor women would cry and take on because their man was in jail, and how they'd work and scrub night and day and nearly kill themselves to earn money to get him out; and then the little childern that come to see their fathers, how they'd stay out of school and work in the packin'-houses and laundries and do any thing for a little money to help them out. Hones'ly I believe if any one stays 'round here for a week he'll see that the people that ain't done nothin' is punished a good deal more'n the others. Why, there was one awful pretty-lookin' girl used to come here to see her father, and the fellers told me that she was studyin' music or somethin' like that, and her father was put in jail on a fine, and she came here to see him every day, and done all she could to earn the money to get him out, but she couldn't do it, and finally she went into one of them sportin' houses down on Clark Street, and lived there long enough to get the money. I don't know, of course, whether it's so, but I don't see why not. Lots of the girls go to the department stores and laundries and stock-yards and they ain't much harder places on a girl's health. Any body'll do everything they can to earn money to save any one they care for.

"Well, the week went away pretty fast. I didn't s'pose 'twas so hard to get a case continued. You know that Carroll case? You remember we quit our work four or five times and lost our pay, and the judge continued it just because the lawyer had somethin' else to do. But I knew 'twouldn't be no use for me to try to get mine continued any more. And I didn't care much. I was gettin' so I'd just about as soon be done with it as not, and still I was pretty sure I'd be hung.

"The next Monday mornin' I was taken into court the same way, and the han'-cuffs was unlocked, and I was set down to the table by my lawyer. One guard set just back of me and the other at the side. Some one started a story that a gang of Bridgeport toughs was comin' to rescue me, but of course there wa'n't nothin' in it. I didn't have a friend that even come to see me—but the newspapers all printed the story, and, of course, that was against me too.

"When the judge called the case, he asked if we was ready, and my lawyer said he needed more time; that he'd done all he could to get ready, but he hadn't had time. But the judge wouldn't pay a bit of attention to him, and said he must go to trial at once, and told the bailiff to call a jury. So the bailiff called the names of twelve men and they took their seats in two rows of chairs along one side of the room. Ever' one of 'em looked at me as if he didn't like to be in the same room where I was. Then the lawyers commenced askin' 'em questions—where they lived, and how long they had lived there, and where they lived before, and how much rent they paid, and what they worked at, and how long they'd worked there, and what they'd done before, and what their fathers done, and where they come from, and was they dead, and if they was married, and how many times, and if they had childern, and how many, and how old, and if they was boys or girls, and if the childern went to school, and what they studied, and if they belonged to the church, and what one, and if they belonged to any societies or lodges or labor unions, or knew any one, or read the papers, or didn't believe in hangin' people, and if they believed in 'circumstantial evidence,' and if they'd hang on circumstantial evidence, and if they believed in the law—and a lot of other things that I can't remember. If any one didn't believe in hangin' he was let go right away; and if they didn't believe in circumstantial evidence they didn't keep 'em either.

"The other lawyer asked questions first and it didn't take him very long to get the ones that he wanted. Ever'one said he believed in hangin', and they all said they'd hang anybody on circumstantial evidence. After he got through my lawyer questioned 'em. They all said that they'd read all about the case, and had formed an opinion about it—and they all looked at me as if they had. Then my lawyer objected to 'em, and the judge said to each one, 'Well, even if you have formed an opinion, don't you think you could lay that aside and not pay any attention to it, and try the case on the evidence and give the prisoner the benefit of the doubt? Don't you think that in spite of the opinion you could presume him innocent when you begin?' Most of 'em said they could; one of 'em said he couldn't. Then the judge lectured him for not bein' able to give any one a fair trial, no matter who he was, and said we'd have to take the others, and told us to go ahead and get another one. So my lawyer tried another one and found him just like the rest. But the judge made us take him anyway. He said they was perfectly fair jurors, and we couldn't expect to get men that sympathized with crime.

"It ain't any use to tell you all about gettin' the jury, and then I hain't got time. Both sides had a right to strike off twenty without any reason at all, only that they didn't like 'em. We took a long time to get a jury. We didn't get much of any until after we had struck off 'most all of our twenty. All the jurors seemed to have made up their minds, but pretty nearly all of 'em said it didn't make any difference; they could give me a fair trial even if their minds was made up.

"I noticed that they struck off workin'-men and Catholics, and people that didn't have any religion, and foreigners, and I noticed my lawyer struck off Baptists, and Presbyterians, and Swedes, and G. A. R.'s. It took three or four days to get the jury, and then we hadn't any more challenges left, and so we had to take 'em. Pretty near ever'one of 'em said they'd read all about the case in all the papers and had their minds made up. I knew, of course, that meant they was against me. But still they all said that didn't make no difference if they had got their minds made up, they could forget their opinions and go at the case as if they believed I was innocent. But ever'one of 'em said he believed in hangin', and all of 'em said that circumstantial evidence was good enough for him. I set there side of the table with my lawyer and looked 'em over, and tried to make up my mind what they was thinkin' of, but they wa'n't one of 'em would look at me when they knew I was lookin', and I could see from the way they did that they was sure all the time that I done it, and ought to swing. Of course, I know it's the law that when a feller's placed on trial they're s'posed to be innocent, but I knew that the judge and all them twelve men felt sure I was guilty or I wouldn't have been there. Of course I done it. I don't know anything that would've done any good, but all the same it's pretty tough to be tried by a jury when they think you ought to be hung before they commence.

"After they got the jury the other lawyer told 'em about the case, and he made it awful black. I don't know how he ever found out all the things he said. Of course a good many of 'em was true and a good many wa'n't true, but he made out that I was the worst man that ever lived. The judge listened to ever' word he said and looked over to me ever' once in a while, as if he wondered how I ever could've done it, and was glad that I was where I belonged at last. The jury watched ever' word the lawyer said, and looked at me ever' once in a while to see how I stood it. Of course it was mighty hard, but I done the best I could. When he got through the judge asked my lawyer what he had to say, and he said he wouldn't tell his side now. Then they commenced puttin' in the evidence.

"I s'pose you read all about it at the time, but the papers always gave me the worst of it, and the evidence wa'n't near so bad as it looked in the papers. Of course they proved about the boy goin' out the next mornin' to the neighbors, and cryin' for his pa and ma, and about ever'one lookin' all over for us without findin' us nor any trace of either one, and about the horse and wagon both lookin' as if it had been out all night. And then the folks as lived next door told about hearin' me say 'you damned bitch,' and hearin' some one fall, though they didn't think much of it then as they'd heard so many rows before. And then they told about findin' a piece of brown paper covered with blood, and then they brought in a doctor, or some one who said he'd examined it with a magnifyin' glass and it was human blood. He wa'n't quite sure whether it was a gentleman or a lady; but he knew 'twas one or the other. Then they brought in the paper and handed it to the jury, and passed it down along both rows, and ever'one took it in his hand and felt it, and looked at it just as if they never had seen any paper like that before, and wanted to make sure 'twas paper and not cloth. Of course the minute I seen it I knew it was the paper that had the beefsteak in it, and I told my lawyer what it was. An I got right up to say something and the judge looked at me just as cross and says 'Set down and keep still; you've got a lawyer to talk for you, and if you say anything more, I'll send you to jail.' Of course I was scart to hear him speak to me that way before the jury and the whole room full of people, and I knew that it would show ever'one that the judge was against me. Some of the papers next day made out that I jumped up and was goin' to run away when I seen the bloody paper.

"My lawyer had another doctor examine a piece of the paper that night, and he said it was a cow or an ox, but he wouldn't come and testify to it unless I'd give him a hunderd dollars, but of course I didn't have that. The court room was awful still when they passed around that paper; you could hear the jurors breathe and they held their heads down as if they felt sorry about somethin'. And after they'd looked it all over the lawyer took it, and the judge says: 'Let me see that paper,' and he put on his spectacles and looked it all over, first on one side and then on the other. He had a little bit of a magnifyin' glass in one hand, and he put it over the paper and looked at it through the glass, and then he looked at me just as solemn as if it was a funeral, and I seen it was all up with me. Of course, I told my lawyer just where I got it and what it was, and he went down to the butcher-shop and seen the man, but the man was 'fraid to come, and said he didn't remember 'bout the steak nor about me; he guessed he'd seen me—I used to come down that way to peddle—but he couldn't tell whether I was in the shop that night or not.

"Then they brought the boys who had found her in a pool of water out on the prairie two or three days after, and they brought some of the clothes she had on. They was all covered with mud, and they passed 'em all around to the jury and the judge, just the same as they did the paper. Of course, these did look pretty bad, and they made me feel kind of faint, for I'd thought about her a good deal the last few days, and dreamed about her almost every night, and sometimes I'd dream that ever'thing was all right, and then wake up and remember just how 'twas. I don't know which is worse: to dream that the thing was done and see it all before you, just as if you were doin' it all over again, and then wake up and know it was a dream, and then know it was so, or to dream that you're livin' together all right and are happy, and then wake up and find that's a dream, and you're in jail for murder and can't never get out alive.

"Then they proved about how the poker just fit into the place in her head, and how it was took back into the kitchen and put into the ashes again, so 'twouldn't show, and how far I drove that day, and ever' saloon I stopped into on the way, and just how much I drank, and ever'thing I done, except the beefsteak I bought and that half peck of potatoes that I gave away to the old lady. Then they proved all about my runnin' away, and where I'd been, and what I'd done, and my changin' my name, and the way I was caught.

"A good many times my lawyer objected to something that they tried to prove, or to something that the other feller was sayin', but ever' time the judge decided 'gainst my lawyer, and he 'most always seemed kind of mad when my lawyer said anything. The other one was a good deal the smartest; ever'one said he wanted to be a judge, and he took all the murder cases he could get, and they called him the 'hangin' lawyer', because ever'one he had anything to do with got hung.

"There was always a big crowd in the court room ever' day, and a lot of people waitin' outside to get in, and there was always some awfully nice dressed ladies settin' up there with the judge ever' day, and they had a sort of glass in their hands, and they'd hold it up in front of their eyes and look at me through the glass just like the judge looked at the paper.

"It took about two days for their side to call all the witnesses they had, and finally their lawyer got up just as solemn and said that was their case.

"Then the judge give them a few minutes recess for ever'body to walk around a little, and ever'one looked at me, just as they'd done all the time. When they come to order the judge told us to go on with our side. My lawyer turned to me and said he didn't see what use it was to prove anything, and we might just as well let the case go the way it was. I said I ought to go on the stand and tell about that paper, and how it was nothin' but the one that come around the beef, and he said they wouldn't believe me if I said it. And anyhow it wouldn't make any difference. If I once got on the stand they'd get me all mixed up and the first thing I knew I'd tell 'em all about ever'thing, and so far as witnesses went he couldn't find any one to do me any good.

"I thought 'twould look pretty bad not to give any evidence at all, and he said he knew that but 'twould look a mighty sight worse if we put any in. So my lawyer got up and ever'one watched to see what he was goin' to do, and then he just said 'May it please the court, we have concluded not to put in any evidence.' And ever'one commenced to whisper, and to look at me, and to look 'round, and the judge looked queer and kind of satisfied, and said then if there was no evidence on our side they would take a recess till mornin' when they could argue the case. Of course, after I went back to the cell and got to thinkin' it over I could see that it was all off more'n ever, but I didn't see that the lawyer could have done any different."

Here Jim got up and went to the grating and called to the guard.

"I'm gettin' a little tired and fagged out and it ain't worth while to go to bed. Won't you just give me some more whiskey?"

The guard came up to the door. "Of course, you can have all the whiskey you want," he said. "Here's a bottle I've just fetched up from the office. You'd better drink that up and then I'll get you some more."

Jim took a long drink at the bottle, and then passed it to his friend. Hank was glad to have something to help him through the ordeal, which had been hard for him to bear.

Presently the guard came back to the grating and asked Jim what he wanted for breakfast.

"It ain't breakfast time yet, is it?" Jim gasped.

"No, but I'm going to the office after a while and I want to give the order when I go. You'd better tell me now. You can have most anything you want. You can have ham and eggs, or bacon or steak, and tea or coffee, and bread and butter and cakes; or all of 'em—or anything else you want."

"Well, I guess you'd better bring me ham and eggs. I don't seem to care for steak, and I don't think I want any coffee. I'd rather have a cocktail. You'd better bring plenty more whiskey too when you come. You know I hain't slept any and I'm kind of nervous. I guess it'll be better if I don't know much about it; don't you?"

"Sure thing," the guard answered back. "We've got some Scotch whiskey over there that's all right. I'll bring you some of that. All the boys takes that. I don't think you'll be troubled much after a good drink of that Scotch. I guess you'd better hurry up a little bit with what you want to say. I don't like to hurry you any, but I'm afraid they'll be along with the breakfast after while, and they don't allow any visitors after that."

The guard turned to leave, but before he had gone far, Jim called out, "You'd better telephone over to the telegraph office, hadn't you? Somethin' might have come maybe."

"All right, I'll do that," the guard answered back, "and Jim, I guess you might as well put on them new clothes before breakfast; they'll look better'n the old ones—to eat in."

X

Jim drank the remnant of whiskey in the bottle he was holding, draining it to the last drop. As he sat in his chair he leaned against the side of the cell.

"My!—how many bottles of this stuff I've drunk to-night. It's a wonder I ain't dead already. I don't believe I could keep up only I've got to finish my story. But this cell begins to swim 'round pretty lively; I guess it ain't goin' to take much to finish me. Think a little of that Scotch will just about do the job. I don't care what any one says, I'm goin' to get just as drunk as I can. I sha'n't live to see what they say in the newspapers and it won't make any difference when I'm dead. I don't know as I ought to eat anything; it might kind of keep it from actin', but still I might as well. I guess the Scotch 'll do it all right anyway.

"Well, there ain't very much more to tell, and I guess you're glad. It's been a tough night on you, poor feller. I hope no one'll ever have to do it for you. But, say—you've done me lots of good! I don't know how I'd put in the night, if you hadn't come!

"Well—the last mornin' they took me over to court, the room was jammed more'n ever before, and a big crowd was waitin' outside. I heard the other lawyer say that the judge's platform looked like a reception; anyhow it was full of ladies with perfectly grand clothes, and most of 'em would hold their glasses up to look at me. The other lawyer didn't say much in his first speech, only to tell how it was all done, and how they had proved that everything happened in Cook County, and what a high office the jury had.

"Then my lawyer talked for me. I didn't really see how he could have done any better and the papers all said he done fine. Of course there wa'n't much to say. I done it, and what more was there to it? And yet I s'pose a lawyer is educated so he can talk all right on either side. Well, my lawyer went on to make out that no one had seen it done, that the evidence was all circumstantial, and no one ever ought to be hung on circumstantial evidence. He went on to show how many mistakes had been made on circumstantial evidence, and he told about a lot of cases. He told the jury about one that I think happened in Vermont where two farmers was seen goin' out in the field. They hadn't been very good friends for a long time. Some one heard loud voices and knew they was fightin'. Finally one of 'em never come back and afterwards some bones or somethin' was found, that the doctors said was a farmer's bones. Well, they tried that farmer and found him guilty, and hung him. And then years afterwards the other man come back. And he'd just wandered off in a crazy fit. And after a while another doctor found out that them bones was only sheep bones, and they'd hung an innocent man. He told a lot of stories of that kind, and some of the jury seemed to cry when he told 'em, but I guess they was cryin' for the Vermont man and not for me.

"After my lawyer got through the other lawyer had one more chance, and he was awful hard on me. He made out that I was the worst man that ever lived. He claimed that I had made up my mind to kill her long ago, just to get rid of her, and that I went 'round to all the saloons that day and drank just to get up my nerve. Then he claimed that I took a bottle of whiskey home and drank it up and left the empty bottle on the table, and I took that just to nerve me up. He made more out of the brown paper than he did of anything else, and told how

I burned all the rest of the evidence but had forgot to burn this, and how I'd gone into the kitchen and got the poker out of the stove and come back into the settin'-room and killed her, and then took it back; and how cold-blooded I was to take her, after I'd killed her, and go and dump her into that hole away out on the prairie, and how I'd run away, and how that proved I'd killed her, and then he compared me with all the murderers who ever lived since Cain, 'most, and showed how all of 'em was better'n I was, and told the jury that nobody in Chicago would be safe unless I was hung; and if they done their duty and hung me there wouldn't be any more killin' in Chicago after this. I can't begin to tell you what all he said; but it was awful! Once in a while when it was too bad, my lawyer would interrupt, but the judge always decided against me and then the other lawyer went on worse'n before. The papers next day told how fast I changed color while he was talkin', and what a great speech he made, and they all said he ought to be a judge because he was so fearless.

"It took the crowd some time to quiet down after he got through, and then the judge asked the jury to stand up, and they stood up, and he read a lot of stuff to 'em, tellin' 'em about the case. 'Most all that he read was 'gainst me. Sometimes I thought he was readin' one on my side, and he told 'em how sure they must be before they could convict, and then he'd wind up by sayin' they must be sure it was done in Cook County. Of course there never was any doubt but what it all happened in Cook County. When the judge got through 'twas most night, and he told the bailiff to take charge of the jury, so he took 'em and the clothes and the brown paper with the blood out in the jury room, and they han'-cuffed me and took me back to my cell.

"I don't believe I ever put in any night that was quite so hard on me—exceptin' mebbe the night I done it—as that one when the jury was out. I guess ever'one thought they wouldn't stay long. I couldn't see that any of 'em ever looked at me once as if they cared whether I lived or died. I don't believe that they really thought I was a man like them; anyhow ever'-one thought they would sentence me to hang in just a few minutes. I s'posed myself that they'd be in before supper. My lawyer come over to the jail with me, because he knew how I felt. And anyhow he was most as nervous as I was. After a while they brought me in my supper, and the lawyer went out to get his. Then the guard told me the jury had gone to supper, and he guessed there was some hitch about it, though ever'one thought the jury wouldn't be out long. After a while the lawyer came back, and he stayed and talked to me until nine or ten o'clock, and the jury didn't come in, so he went to see what was the matter, and come back and said he couldn't find out anything, only that they hadn't agreed.

"Well, he stayed till twelve o'clock, and then the judge went home, and we knew they wa'n't goin' to come in till mornin'. I couldn't sleep that night, but walked back and forth in the cell a good bit of the time. You see it wa'n't this cell. The one I had then was a little bigger. I'd lay down once in a while, and sometimes I'd smoke a cigar that the guard gave me. Anyhow I couldn't really sleep, and was mighty glad when daylight come. In the mornin', kind of early, I heard that the jury had agreed and I knew that 'twas bad for me. The best that could happen would be a disagreement. I hadn't allowed myself to have much hope any of the time, but I knew that now it was all off.

"Still I waited and didn't quite give up till they took me back to the courtroom. Then when ever'one had got their places the jury come in, lookin' awful solemn, and the judge looked sober and fierce-like, and he said, 'Gentlemen of the Jury, have you agreed on your verdict?' And the foreman got up and said, 'We have.' Then the judge told the foreman to give the verdict to the clerk. He walked over to the row of chairs and the man at the end of the bottom row reached out his hand and gave the paper to him. The people in the room was still as death. Then the clerk read, 'We, the jury, find the defendant guilty, and sentence him to death.' I set with my head down, lookin' at the paper; I expected it, and made up my mind not to move. Ever'one in the courtroom sort of give a sigh. I never looked up, and I don't believe I moved. The papers next day said I was brazen and had no feelin', even when the jury sentenced me to death.

"The judge was the first one to speak. He turned to the jury and thanked 'em for their patriotism and devotion, and the great courage they'd shown by their verdict. He said they'd done their duty well and could now go back to their homes contented and happy. And he says: 'Mr. Sheriff, remove the prisoner from the room.' Of course, I hadn't expected nothin', and still I wa'n't quite sure—the same as now, when I think mebbe the governor 'll change his mind. But when the verdict was read and they said it was death, somehow I felt kind of dazed. I don't really remember their puttin' the han'-cuffs on me, and takin' me back to jail. I don't remember the crowd in the court-room, or much of anything until I was locked up again, and then my lawyer come and said he would make a motion for a new trial, and not to give up hope. My lawyer told me that the reason they was out so long was one man stuck out for sendin' me to the penitentiary for life instead of hangin' me. We found out that he used to be a switchman. I s'pose he knew what a hard life I had and wanted to make some allowances. The State's Attorney said he'd been bribed, and the newspapers had lots to say about investigatin' the case, but there wa'n't nothin' done about it. But I s'pose mebbe it had some effect on the next case.

"There wa'n't nothin' more done for two or three days. I just stayed in my cell and didn't feel much like talkin' with any one. Then my lawyer come over and said the motion for a new trial would be heard next day. In the mornin' they han'cuffed me and took me back as usual. There was a lot of people in the courtroom, though not so many as before. My lawyer had a lot of books, and he talked a long while about the case, and told the judge he ought to give me a new trial on account of all the mistakes that was made before. And after he got done the judge said he'd thought of this case a great deal both by day and by night, and he'd tried to find a way not to sentence me to death, but he couldn't do it, and the motion would be overruled. Then he said, 'Jackson, stand up.' Of course I got up, because he told me to. Then he looked at me awful savage and solemn and said 'Have you got anything to say why sentence should not be passed on you?' and I said 'No!' Then he talked for a long time about how awful bad I was, and what a warnin' I ought to be to ever'body else; and then he sentenced me to be removed to the county-jail and on Friday, the thirteenth day of this month—that's to-day—to be hanged by the neck till dead, and then he said, 'May God have mercy on your soul!' After that he said, 'Mr. Sheriff, remove the prisoner. Mr. Clerk, call the next case.' And they han'-cuffed me and brought me back.

"I don't know why the judge said, 'May God have mercy on your soul!' I guess it was only a kind of form that they have to go through, and I don't think he meant it, or even thought anything about it. If he had, I don't see how he really could ask God to have mercy on me unless he could have mercy himself. The judge didn't have to hang me unless he wanted to.

"Well, the lawyer come in and told me he ought to appeal the case to the Supreme Court, but it would cost one hundred dollars for a record, and he didn't know where to get the money. I told him I didn't know either. Of course I hadn't any, and told him he might just as well let it go; that I didn't s'pose it would do any good anyhow. But he said he'd see if he could find the money somehow and the next day he come in and said he was goin' to give half out of his own pocket, and he'd seen another feller that didn't want his name mentioned and that thought a man oughtn't to be hung without a chance; he was goin' to give the other half. Of course I felt better then, but still I thought there wa'n't much chance, for ever'body was against me, but my lawyer told me there was a lot of mistakes and errors in the trial and I ought to win.

"Well, he worked on the record and finally got it finished, a great big kind of book that told all about the case. It was only finished a week ago, and I s'posed any one could take his case to the Supreme Court if he had the money; but my lawyer said no, he couldn't, or rather he said yes, any one could take his case to the Supreme Court, but in a case like mine, where I was to be hung I'd be dead before the Supreme Court ever decided it, or even before it was tried. Then he said the only way would be if some of the judges looked at the record and made an order that I shouldn't be hung until after they'd tried the case, but he told me it didn't make any difference how many mistakes the judge had made, or how many errors there was, they wouldn't make any order unless they believed I hadn't done it. He said that if it had been a dispute about a horse or a cow, or a hundred dollars, I'd have a right to go to the Supreme Court, and if the judges found any mistakes in the trial I'd have another chance. But it wa'n't so when I was tried for my life.

"Well, when he'd explained this I felt sure 'twas all off, and I told him so, but he said he was goin' to make the best fight he could and not give up till the end. He said he had a lot at stake himself, though not so much as I had. So he took the record and went to the judges of the Supreme Court and they looked it over, and said mebbe the judge that tried me did make some mistakes, and mebbe I didn't have a fair trial, but it looked as if I was guilty and they wouldn't make any order. So my case never got into the Supreme Court after all and the hundred dollars was wasted.

"Well, when my lawyer told me, of course I felt blue. I'd built some on this, and it begun to look pretty bad. It seemed as if things was comin' along mighty fast, and it looked as if the bobbin was most wound up. When you know you're goin' to die in a week the time don't seem long. Of course if a feller's real sick, and gets run down and discouraged, and hasn't got much grip on things, he may not feel so very bad about dyin', for he's 'most dead anyway, but when a feller's strong, and in good health, and he knows he's got to die in a week, it's a different thing.

"Then my lawyer said there was only one thing left, and that was to go to the gov'nor. He said he knew the gov'nor pretty well and he was goin' to try. He thought mebbe he'd change the sentence to imprisonment for life. When I first come to jail I said I'd rather be hung than to be sent up for life, and I stuck to it even when the jury brought in their verdict, but when it was only a week away I begun to feel different, and I didn't want to die, leastwise I didn't want to get hung. So I told him all the people I knew, though I didn't think they'd help me, for the world seemed to be against me, and the papers kept tellin' what a good thing it was to hang me, and how the State's Attorney and the jury and the judge had been awful brave to do it so quick. But I couldn't see where there was any bravery in it. I didn't have no friends. It might have been right, but I can't see where the brave part come in.

"But every day the lawyer said he thought the gov'nor would do somethin', and finally he got all the names he could to the petition, and I guess it wa'n't very many, only the people that sign all the petitions because they don't believe in hangin'; and day before yesterday, he went down to Springfield to see the gov'nor.

"Well, I waited all day yesterday. I didn't go out of the cell for exercise because I couldn't do anything and I didn't want 'em to see how nervous I was. But I tell you it's ticklish business waitin' all day when you're goin' to be hung in the mornin' unless somethin' happens. I kep' askin' the guard what time 'twas, and when I heard any one comin' up this way I looked to see if it wa'n't a despatch, and I couldn't set down or lay down, or do anything 'cept drink whiskey. I hain't really been sober and clear-headed since yesterday noon, in fact, I guess if I had been, I wouldn't kep' you here all night like this. I didn't hardly eat a thing, either, all day, and I asked the guard about it a good many times, and he felt kind of sorry for me but didn't give me much encouragement. You see they've had a guard right here in front of the door all the time, day and night, for two weeks. That's called the death watch, and they set here to see that I don't kill myself, though I can't see why that would make any great difference so long as I've got to die anyhow.

"Well, 'long toward night the guard came and brought me that new suit of clothes over on the bed, and I guess I've got to put 'em on pretty quick. Of course, the guard's been as nice as he could be. He didn't tell me what they's for, but I knew all the same. I know they don't hang nobody in their old clothes. I s'pose there'll be a good many people there, judges and doctors and ministers and lawyers, and the newspapers, and the friends of the sheriff, and politicians, and all, and of course it wouldn't look right to have me hung up there before 'em all in my old clothes,—it would be about like wearin' old duds to a party or to church—so I've got to put on them new ones. They're pretty good, and they look as if they're all wool, don't you think?

"Well, a little while after they brought me the clothes, I seen the guard come up with a telegram in his hand. I could see in his face it wa'n't no use, so of course I wa'n't quite so nervous when I read it. But I opened it to make sure. The lawyer said that the gov'nor wouldn't do nothin'. Then, of course, 'twas all off. Still he said he'd go back about midnight. I don't know whether he meant it, or said it to brace me up a little and kind of let me down easier.

"Of course, the gov'nor could wake up in the night and do it, if he wanted to, and I s'pose such things has been done. I've read 'bout 'em stoppin' it after a man got up on the scaffold. You remember about the gov'nor of Ohio, don't you? He come here to Chicago to some convention, and a man was to be hung in Columbus that day, and the gov'nor forgot it till just about the time, and then he tried for almost an hour to get the penitentiary on the long distance telephone, and he finally got 'em just as the man was goin' up on the scaffold. Such things has happened, but of course, I don't s'pose they'll happen to me. I never had much luck in anything, and I guess I'll be hung all right.

"It seems queer, don't it, how I'm talkin' to you here, and the guard out there, and ever'body good to me, and in just a little while they're goin' to take me out there and hang me! I don't believe I could do it, even if I was a sheriff and got ten thousand dollars a year for it, but I s'pose it has to be done.

"Well, now I guess I've told you all about how ever'thing happened and you und'stand how it was. I s'pose you think I'm bad, and I don't want to excuse myself too much, or make out I'm any saint. I know I never was, but you see how a feller gets into them things when he ain't much different from ever'body else. I know I don't like crime, and I don't believe the others does. I just got into a sort of a mill and here I am right close up to that noose.

"There ain't any one 'specially that I've got to worry about, 'cept the boy. Of course it's awful hard for a poor feller to start, anyhow, unless he's real smart, and I don't know how 'twill be with the boy. We always thought he was awful cunnin'; but I s'pose most parents does. But I don't see how he'd ever be very smart 'cause I wa'n't and neither was his mother. As I was sayin', 'twould be awful hard for him anyhow, but now when he's growed up, and any one tells him about how his mother was murdered by his father, and how his father got hung for it, and they show him the pictures in the paper and all that, I don't see how he'll ever have any show. It seems as if the state had ought to do somethin' for a child when the state kills its father that way, but it don't unless they sends him to a poor house, or something like that.

"Now, I haven't told you a single lie—and you can see how it all was, and that I wa'n't so awful bad, and that I'm sorry, and would be willin' to die if it would bring her back. And if you can, I wish you'd just kind of keep your eye on the boy. I guess it'll be a good deal better to change his name and not let him nor any one else know anything about either of us. A good many poor people grow up that way. I don't really know nothin' 'bout my folks. They might've been hung too, for all I know. But you kind of watch the boy and keep track of him, and if he comes up all right and seems to be a smart feller and looks at things right, and he gets to wonderin' about me, and you think 'twill do any good you can tell him just what you feel a mind to, but don't tell him 'less'n you think it will do him good. Of course, I can't never pay you in any way for what you've done for me, but mebbe you'll think it's worth while for a feller that hain't a friend in the world, and who's got to be hung so quick."

Hank struggled as hard as he could to keep back the tears. He was not much used to crying, but in spite of all his efforts they rolled down his face.

"Well, Jim, old feller," he said. "I didn't know how it was—when I come I felt as if you'd been awful bad, and of course I know it wa'n't right, but somehow I know it might have happened to me, or most anybody, almost, and that you ain't so bad. I can't tell you anything about how I feel, but I'm glad I come. It's done me good. I don't think I'll ever feel the same about the fellers that go to jail and get hung. I don't know's they could help it any more'n any of us can help the things we do. Anyhow, I sha'n't never let the boy out of my mind a single minit, and I'll do as much for him as if he was mine. I'll look him up the first thing I do. I don't know about changin' his name, I'll see. Anyhow, if he ever gets to hear a bit of it, I'll see he knows how it was."

Jim wrung Hank's hand for a minute in silence, and then said: "And just one word more, Hank; tell him not to be poor; don't let him get married till he's got money, and can afford it, and don't let him go in debt. You know I don't believe I ever would have done it if I hadn't been so poor."

Hank drew back his hand and stepped to the grated door and looked out along the gloomy iron corridors and down toward the courtyard below. Then he looked up at the tiers of cells filled with the hapless outcasts of the world. On the skylight he could see the faint yellowish glow that told him that the day was about to dawn. The guard got up from his stool and passed him another flask of whiskey.

"Here, you'd better get Jim to drink all he can," he whispered, "for his time is almost up."

Hank took a little sip himself, and then motioned Jim to drink. Jim took the bottle, raised it to his mouth and gulped it down, scarcely stopping to catch his breath. Then he threw the bottle on the bed and sat down on his chair. With the story off his mind it was plain that the whiskey was fast numbing all his nerves. He was not himself when he looked up again.

"I guess mebbe I'd better change my clothes,

while I have a chance," he said. "I don't want any one else to have to do it for me, and I want to look all right when the thing comes off."

A new guard came up to the door, unlocked it and came in. He nodded to Hank and told him he must go.

"His breakfast is just comin' up and it's against the rules to have any one here at the time. The priest will come to see him after he gets through eatin'."

Over in the corridor where Hank had seen the beams and lumber he could hear the murmur of muffled voices, evidently talking about the work. Along the corridor two waiters in white coats were bringing great trays filled with steaming food.

Slowly Hank turned to Jim and took his hand.

"Well, old fellow," he said, "I've got to go. I see you're all right, but take that Scotch whiskey when it comes; it won't do you any hurt. I'll look after everything just as I said. Good-bye."

Jim seemed hardly to hear Hank's farewell words.

"Well, good-bye."

Hank went outside the door and the guard closed and locked it as he turned away.

Then Jim got up from his chair and stumbled to the door.

"Hank! Hank! S'pose—you—stop at the—telegraph—office—the Western Union—and the —Postal—all of 'em—mebbe—might—be some-thin'——"

"All right," Hank called back, "I will! I will!—I'll go to both to make sure if there's anything there; and I'll telephone you by the time you've got through eatin."

Reprints of Legal Classics Published by
ꕤ *The Lawbook Exchange, Ltd.* ꕤ

The following titles may obtained from your bookseller or by contacting:

The Lawbook Exchange, Ltd.
965 Jefferson Avenue
Union, New Jersey 07083-8605

Telephone: (908) 686-1998 or (800) 422-6686
Fax: (908) 686-3098
E-Mail: lawbkexc@haven.ios.com
Web Site: http://www.abaa-booknet.com/usa/lbe/

Legal Treatises

1. Pomeroy's Treatise on Equity Jurisprudence. [Fifth Edition]. *John N. Pomeroy. Edited by Spencer W. Symons.* Five volumes. 914; 1134; 1063; 1104; 716 pp. 1941. Reprinted 1995. ISBN 1-886363-05-6. $450.

* Limited to 100 sets. By special permission of the publisher. "Few modern textbooks are of permanent value. Pomeroy's *Equity Jurisprudence* is an exception." Albert J. Beveridge in Vanderbilt, *Studying Law*, p. 27. "As a book of reference, indeed, it will outrank the *Restatements*.... As an encyclopedia, too, Pomeroy is useful as indicating some of the reaches of our equitable process." *Virginia Law Review*, 29:507-9.

2. Freeman on Judgments. [Fifth edition]. *A.C. Freeman. Edited by Edward W. Tuttle.* Three volumes. 1216; 1280; 1264 pp. 1925. Reprinted 1993. ISBN 0-9630106-6-2. $295.

* Limited to 100 sets. By special permission of the publisher. Considered by Vanderbilt to be one of the great textbooks in which "the history of American law might well be traced." *Men and Measures in the Law*, p. 21. "In the present treatise (which cites over 35,000 cases), the editor has analyzed the cases with care.... The book will be of great assistance to lawyers searching for authorities in the important field it covers. *Harvard Law Review* 32(2):283-5.

3. Notes on the Science of Government and the Relations of the States to the United States. *Raleigh C. Minor.* x, 192 pp. 1913. Reprinted 1995. ISBN 1-886363-09-9. $40.

* Minor (1869-1923) was an author, publicist, and teacher of law at the University of Virginia, where his father was only the fourth to become professor of law. Minor continued his father's excellence in legal education and was a pioneer in private international law or the conflict of laws. In his *Notes*, Minor presents a thorough overview of both government in general and the relationship of states to the federal government. Anyone interested in the question of states' rights a debate that remains ongoing will find much of value in Minor's analysis of the legal status of the states and federal government under the Constitution. After developing the basic features of government, Minor elaborates upon the States Rights and Nationalistic schools of thought, drawing upon numerous Supreme Court cases and the writings of Story, de Tocqueville, Webster, Calhoun, Madison, and others.

4. The Evolution of the Constitution of the United States. Showing That It Is a Development of Progressive History and Not an Isolated Document Struck Off at a Given Time or an Imitation of English or Dutch Forms of Government. *Sydney George Fisher.* 398 pp. 1897. Reprinted 1996.ISBN 1-886363-08-0. $50.

* Fisher (1856-1927) was a prominent historian and lawyer, who was admitted to the Pennsylvania bar in 1883 after legal studies at Harvard University. His *Evolution of the Constitution* collates for the first time all the various provisions of colonial documents that served as source material for the Constitution. Asserting that the Constitution was neither an imitation nor an invention, Fisher traces every material clause back to its origin. Twenty-nine colonial charters and constitutions, seventeen Revolutionary constitutions, and twenty-three plans of union are the resulting source materials from which Fisher draws his analysis. Abundant quotations from the sixty-nine documents illustrate the evolutionary nature of the Constitution and make this a valuable sourcebook for the reader who desires to find in one volume the Constitution's many and varied origins.

5. Historians of Anglo-American Law. *W.H. Holdsworth.* 175 pp. 1928. Reprinted 1994. ISBN 0-9630106-9-7. $40.

* In chronological order, beginning with Coke and Selden, Holdsworth surveys the work of the great practitioners of Anglo-American legal history. No one interested in the growth of Anglo-American law can fail to read with

pleasure and profit this stimulating treatment of the development of legal history.

6. History of Trial by Jury. [Second edition]. *William Forsyth.* x, 388 pp. [1875]. Reprinted 1994. ISBN 0-9630106-8-9. $50.

* First published in England in 1852, Forsyth's *Trial by Jury* is the first full-scale historical account of the rise and growth of the jury system in England. The American edition adds a number of notes, as well as making several corrections to American references.

7. Select Essays in Anglo-American Legal History. *By Maitland, Pollock, Holmes, Beale, Holdsworth and Others. Compiled and Edited by a Committee of the Association of American Law Schools.* Three volumes. 1907-1909. Reprinted 1992. LC 91-77977. ISBN 0-9630106-0-1. $195.

* Originally conceived as a companion volume to Pollock & Maitland's *History of English Law*, this valuable work of legal scholarship, long out-of-print, has become increasingly difficult to obtain. Its 76 essays fill some 2,500 pages. At the time of its original publication the *Harvard Law Review* stated: "No one can fail to be impressed with the deep research, the deliberate construction, and the substantial worth of these essays." A detailed table of contents is available upon request.

Legal Dictionaries

8. Bouvier's Law Dictionary. [First edition]. John Bouvier. Two volumes. 559; 628 pp., 1839. Reprinted 1993. ISBN 0-9630106-7-0.$130.

* First American law dictionary to be published. Long recognized as a leading authority, all other American law dictionaries are inevitably compared with this one. A concise encyclopedia of Anglo-American law, its outstanding feature is its emphasis on the American elements in the law. The original volumes are quit rare, RLIN showing only two locations.

9. Tayler's Law Glossary. Being a Selection of the the Greek, Latin, Saxon, French, Norman and Italian Sentences, Phrases, and Maxims, Found in the Leading English and American Reports, and Elementary Works. [Fourth Edition]. Thomas Tayler. 580 pp. 1856. Reprinted 1995. ISBN 1-886363-12-9. $65.

* This early dictionary offers a unique historical perspective on the state of American law in the mid-eighteenth century. It contains translations of nearly

five-thousand items of foreign origin and supplies definitions for innumerable maxims of law found in both English and American sources. The author has paid great attention to the context of legal terms and supplies extensive notes, with citations, after each section of his glossary (i.e., after "A", "B", "C", etc.). This glossary is an important research tool that will aid greatly in elucidating both the source and meaning of legal concepts of the last century.

10. Black's Law Dictionary. [First Edition]. *Henry Campbell Black.* x, 1253 pp. 1891. Reprinted 1991. LC 91-62383. ISBN 0-9630106-0-3. $125.

* Reprint of the rare first edition of the classic American Law Dictionary, now in its sixth edition. Contains definitions of the terms and phrases of American and English jurisprudence, ancient and modern (including the principal terms of international, constitutional, and commercial law). There is also a collection of legal maxims, as well as a bibliography of the principal law dictionaries in English and other languages to 1891.

11. Black's Law Dictionary. [Second Edition]. *Henry Campbell Black.* 1314 pp. 1910. Reprinted 1995. ISBN 1-886363-10-2. $125.
* The second edition of Black's classic dictionary incorporates many new definitions and additional citations to decided cases, besides being a thorough revision of previous entries. Also included are many Latin and French terms overlooked in the first edition. Medical jurisprudence in particular is enriched, with new definitions for insanity and pathological and criminal insanity. The second edition (1910) is an essential complement to the first edition (1891) as it provides the scholar and student of law important insights into the rapid development of law at the turn of the century. The second edition is also notable for its revamped system of arrangement, with all compound and descriptive terms subsumed under their related main entries. Libraries, students, historians, and practitioners will all benefit from this historically significant research tool.

☙ *Legal Bibliography & Reference* ❧

12. A Complete List of British and Colonial Law Reports and Legal Periodicals. Arranged in Alphabetical and in Chronological Order with Bibliographical Notes. With a Check List of Canadian Statutes. [Third Edition]. *W. Harold Maxwell and C.R. Brown.* viii, 141, 49 pp. 1937. Reprinted 1995. ISBN 1-886363-11-0. $70.

* This comprehensive guide includes every known edition of every British or

Colonial law report (except American reprints). This edition also includes a list of the various territories in the British Empire which had issued printed legislation. Librarians and scholars will find this a particularly useful checklist, with notes that supplement Soule's earlier *Lawyer's Reference Manual.*

13. Men and Books Famous in the Law. *Frederick C. Hicks.* 259 pp. 1921. Reprinted 1992. LC 92-070809. ISBN 0-9630106-2-X. $50.
* A classic account of law books and their authors. Within the pages of this volume will be found the stories of great legal writers, and more especially the story of their legal writings, the inception, production, and vicissitudes of works which have become classics of legal literature. Covers the lives and publications of Littleton, Coke, Blackstone, Cowell, Kent, Wheaton and Livingston.

14. The William Blackstone Collection in the Yale Law Library. A Bibliographical Catalogue. *Catherine Spicer Eller.* 134 pp. 1938. Reprinted 1993. ISBN 0-9630106-5-4. $40.
* The *William Blackstone Collection* bibliography is primarily a description of the *Blackstoniana* in the Yale Law Library and the Yale University Library, but with additional information concerning editions not held by Yale. It is believed to describe the most comprehensive collection of editions and abridgments of the Commentaries to be found in any one library. Friend, *Anglo-American Legal Bibliographies*, p. 69. Includes not only the Commentaries, but all legal works of William Blackstone, as well as pertinent criticism.

15. Ragbag of Legal Quotations. *Compiled by M. Frances McNamara.* [xi], 334 pp. 1960. Reprinted 1992. LC 92-074141. ISBN 0-9630106-3-8. $50.
* One of the best collections of legal quotations ever. McNamara's attractive and well-indexed volume provides over 2,000 quotations arranged under nearly 300 subject headings, which are further indexed by author and by words and phrases. Explanatory notes clarify the meaning of some well-known, but misunderstood quotations.

16. Latin for Lawyers. With 1000 Legal Maxims. *E. Hilton Jackson.* [viii], 300 pp. 1915. Reprinted 1992. LC 92-074408. ISBN 0-9630106-4-6. $50.
* The perfect book for that considerable number of law students and lawyers with no knowledge of Latin, who would like to acquire a little to aid them in their profession. For those who already know some Latin, their interest in this

volume will lie in the large collection of legal maxims and phrases. The annotations are commendable for their brevity and unpretentious simplicity.

℘ *Law & Literature* ℘

17. Charles Dickens As a Legal Historian. *William S. Holdsworth.* 157 pp. 1928. Reprinted 1995. ISBN 1-886363-0.6-4. $40.

* "The distinguished English historian, Professor Holdsworth, has contrived even during his moments of recreation to render us his debtors. No two books outside the bounds of technical law are more worth reading for law students than *Pickwick Papers* and *Bleak House*. Even a trained trial lawyer however, is puzzled by some of the legal points brought up by Dickens, because they have fortunately passed forever out of the realm of living law. Professor Holdsworth has performed a valuable service to lawyers and laymen alike in explaining these obscurities. And he has done much more than this. He has increased our admiration for the genius of Dickens by proving his great merit as a legal historian.... Although some of the information in this book has already appeared in the author's great *History of English Law*, it derives an increased force from the picturesque material with which it is surrounded. All lawyers and all lovers of Dickens will be wise in reading Professor Holdsworth's book." Zechariah Chafee, Jr. *Harvard Law Review* 42:286-8.

18. An Eye for an Eye. *Clarence S. Darrow.* 213 pp. 1905. Reprinted 1996. ISBN 1-886363-07-2. $40.

* *An Eye for an Eye* was Darrow's only fictional work, aside from his autobiographical novel, *Farmington*, published in 1904.It tells the story of Jim Jackson, who struggles with poverty and harsh circumstances, before finally murdering his wife in a fit of rage. Faced with the gallows, Jackson confesses: "If ther'd been forty scaffolds right before my eyes, I'd have brought down the poker just the same." Darrow's novel is a sociological polemic which foreshadows later such works as Theodore Dreiser's *An American Tragedy* and Upton Sinclair's *The Jungle.* Reviewing *An Eye for an Eye* for the *Bookman* (February 1906), Isabel Colbron stated: "If to create an illusion, to attain the effect aimed at, completely and entirely, is literary art, then Mr. Darrow's work is literary art of the highest, in spite of an apparenct neglect of all the canons of literary art." Abe Ravitz in his *Clarence Darrow and the American Literary Tradition* (1962), observed that *An Eye for an Eye* was worthy of "a trophy not only for sociological veracity but also for genuine literary achievement."